make your own
digital photo
scrapbook

make your own
digital photo
scrapbook

Roger Pring and Ivan Hissey

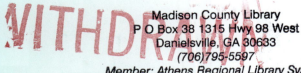

An Ilex Press Book
Friedman/Fairfax Publishers
Please visit the website: www.metrobooks.com

This edition published by Friedman/Fairfax by
arrangement with The Ilex Press Limited
2002 Friedman/Fairfax Publishers
Copyright © 2002 The Ilex Press Limited

A CIP record for this book is available from
the Library of Congress

This book was conceived, designed, and produced
by The Ilex Press Limited, The Barn, College Farm,
1 West End, Whittlesford, Cambridge CB2 4LX England
Sales office: The Old Candlemakers, West Street,
Lewes, East Sussex BN7 2NZ England

Publisher: Alastair Campbell
Executive Publisher: Sophie Collins
Creative Director: Peter Bridgewater
Editorial Director: Steve Luck
Art Director: Tony Seddon

Editor: Chris Middleton
Illustrator and Photographer: Ivan Hissey
Contributors: Roger Pring, Peter Cope, Chris Middleton
Designer: Alistair Plumb

ISBN 1-586-63712-6

Distributed by Sterling Publishing Company, Inc.
387 Park Avenue South
New York, NY 10016

Distributed in Canada by
Sterling Publishing
Canadian Manda Group
One Atlantic Avenue, Suite 105
Toronto, Ontario, Canada M6K 3E7

*For updated weblinks and up-to-date information on digital photography,
please visit: www.digital-photo-scrapbook.com*

Contents

It's time to throw away the scissors and glue

Scrapbooks used to be about scissors, paper, and glue. But today digital technology can be used to bring your family photos and memorabilia—your memories, in fact—to life in ways that were unimaginable just a few years ago. So if you've got a computer and an Internet connection (even if it's just your normal phone line) plus a bit of imagination, then you can transform your ancestors' photos, your vacation souvenirs, your videos of family and friends, even children's drawings and snapshots of pets, into an interactive experience that you can publish online, put onto CD, or email your friends—wherever in the world they might be!

You don't need to have all the latest equipment; just a computer (it doesn't matter if it's a PC or a Mac), a printer —and that Internet connection.

You'll also need to have some way of getting your snaps onto your computer. If you have a digital still or video camera, then that's ideal; if not, you'll need a scanner.

A CD writer (either built into your computer or external) would help, but there are ways around this if you don't have one yet. But remember: all this kind of equipment is getting cheaper by the day, so the investment might not be as large as you think!

So let's get started. By the end of this book you'll have mastered the techniques, not just of preserving your favorite mementoes and immortalizing those special memories, but also of giving them a new lease of life. The Internet is truly a global network, and it's growing by the second: why not be part of it and share your passions and memories with the people you care about the most, wherever they happen to be? And maybe you could make new contacts and friends in the process... they're all out there at the click of a mouse. We'll show you how to do all this and much, much more. But first, here's the science part... then it's on to the projects. Got your ideas ready? Let's go!

All you need to know about...

This book is all about the fun projects you can do with a bit of imagination, a computer, a camera, and some other neat pieces of digital technology. But you may be thinking, "I don't know anything about computers, or the Internet!" Well, we've got news for you: neither do most people; they just like what digital technology can do for them! And you will too, if you follow the projects. But first, here's a quick run-through of what the technology is, and what it does...

Inside your computer

Always at the cutting edge of hardware and operating system design, Apple's iMac has quickly become a design icon. More importantly for you, it has some neat, built-in image-handling talents. In fact, like most Apple products, its favorite job is handling digital images. With a FireWire connection, you'll soon be flying!

If you already know your way around the inside of your computer, skip this introduction. But if you want to find out more about it and some of the other gadgets you might have invested in to go with it, then read on. It will help you get the most out of the projects later in the book.

The chances are that your computer, if it's a fairly recent design, already has the built-in capabilities for most of the creative stuff we've got lined up for you. And when you need to add new items, like extra memory or a scanner, we'll show you how—and what they're capable of!

Getting the information in

So, how do you get the pictures in? There are three main methods. The first option is to connect a digital camera directly to an input socket on the computer, or take the storage card from the camera and slot it into a card reader (which is in turn connected to the computer). If you don't have any of these, don't worry. Many perfectly good digital cameras are comparatively cheap nowadays, and prices are falling all the time as the technology improves.

But if you don't want to make the investment, there are other options, such as using a scanner. Any picture or document—or even a small object that can be placed (carefully!) on the scanner glass—is easily captured and fed directly into your computer.

If you don't have a scanner (you'll find they're fairly inexpensive) you could always use your computer's built-in CD drive to input images from a PhotoCD, as well as from commercial clip-art and photo collections.

With today's computers and the Internet, there's literally a whole world of possibilities out there for creative minds. And unlike a paper-based scrapbook or photo album, you'll find all your pictures, text, and memorabilia can be almost infinitely changed, updated—and preserved in time.

Beyond this, why not use your email connection to swap your own pictures with friends and family? There are also millions of copyright-free pictures you could download from the Internet (but make sure they really are copyright-free before distributing them to your friends!).

As technology prices drop, even a computer as small and portable as this recent Dell laptop has the speed, memory, and processing power to handle digital images with ease.

By far the most common hardware and software platform, the Windows PC has grabbed the world's attention over the last decade. Because it's so common—well over three-quarters of the world's wired population has one—you can be sure nearly all the software and hardware you buy will be compatible with it. This high-end Sony Vaio model (also available in laptop versions) is designed for the kind of work we'll be doing. That digital video camera plugs right in...

Storage and memory

Computers are highly organized machines, and you'll need to be ultra-organized when it comes to picture filing, so that all the projects you embark on work quickly and easily. But where does all the information get stored? While they're being worked on, your pictures are held temporarily in what's called RAM (Random Access Memory). When the job's done, it's stored on your hard drive or disk (actually a stack of magnetic disks, with tiny reading and writing heads between the disks).

You'll come across lots of computing terms and abbreviations once you start using your computer and the Internet regularly. One example is the different types of memory referred to above. The capacity of both is measured in Megabytes, and this is often used to compare the capability of one computer with another. Luckily, recent technology has come to the rescue. While your computer might typically have 128 or 256 Megabytes (Mb) of RAM, its hard drive may have 40,000 to 60,000 Megabytes of storage space—now handily described as 40 or 60 Gigabytes (Gb).

But why is all this important? Well, the point to remember is that more RAM lets you work with more powerful software, while more storage, not surprisingly, lets you keep more of the resulting work on your hard drive. If even this amount of storage proves insufficient, it might be time to invest in peripheral storage devices (see page 22).

The processor

Otherwise known as the CPU, the central processing unit is where all the calculating power of the computer is concentrated. It doesn't matter whether the computer is working out your tax return, improving the color of your Christmas photographs, or building a webpage, the same circuitry is processing information at breakneck speed. The actual speed (the "clock" speed) is expressed in Megahertz (MHz) and Gigahertz, and there is a continuous scramble among manufacturers to attain the highest rating. Apple's Macintosh hardware works slightly differently.

The screen

Although capable of showing much higher resolution, the conventional computer monitor is much like your TV screen. The same three guns at the back of the tube fire precise patterns of electrons, red, green, and blue, at phosphors coating the inside of the screen. This technology is being superseded by LCD (Liquid Crystal Display) monitors, which offer less bulk and improved economy.

Getting the information out

Color inkjet printers now promise near-photographic quality on a huge variety of papers. The final picture appearance is influenced by the resolution of the image (see page 15), although most printer software allows you to vary the quality of the output, with a trade-off of speed against resolution.

All about software

Your computer arrived with its own basic operating program built in. This "system" software takes care of all the fundamental tasks like starting up the computer, sorting documents, connecting to add-on ("peripheral") hardware like printers, scanners, and digital cameras—and finally shutting the system down at the end of a session. It runs quietly in the background and, with luck on your side, you need never notice it. More recent machines have more stable operating systems, but they all do the same basic job.

Beyond the basics

To do any useful work, you need more software. As a minimum, you need to be able to organize, size, trim, and enhance your pictures. The choice of software is vast and growing almost daily. If you want to change the color of the paint on the back porch in that old photo from the 1970s, insert an absent family member into an existing group photo, reduce the effect of those telltale wrinkles, or wrap your vacation pictures around an animated globe, there are programs competing for your dollar. And each software package encourages you to follow the inevitable, and costly, upgrade path.

Take a moment to reflect on your choice. Maybe start with a basic "image-editing" program. Something like Photoshop Elements (available for both Windows and Apple Mac machines) gives you the power to do basic photo retouching and correcting (including removal of the inevitable "red eye"), merge one picture with another, create a complete photo story, and finally produce prints, emails, or webpages. This program is available in a try-out version (you get 30 days of free use) as a download from the Adobe website. See page 18 to check out the whole business of Internet connection. If you'd rather not get involved with all that technology, find a friend who is already equipped, and persuade him or her to download it for you. At around 70 Megabytes (Mb) in size, it shouldn't take too long to download on a cable or broadband connection. If any of these terms seems mysterious, see page 152 for a detailed explanation.

What about the words?

You'll probably have a simple wordprocessing program on your machine, but it may limit your freedom of choice in terms of layout and design. At the other end of the scale, full-size wordprocessing programs such as Microsoft Word (which you may also have preinstalled) offer greater control over every aspect of type handling, and you can easily import your pictures so they sit right in the page alongside the words. You may find that the number of functions available is overwhelming. There's usually an escape hatch provided in the form of a set of templates where many of the necessary decisions have been taken already—leaving you to feed your material into predetermined slots. See page 28 for a typical project using a wordprocessing program like this. You'll also find your computer has a range of different typefaces (lettering styles, or "fonts") built into its operating system.

They're mostly plain and utilitarian, but it's easy to add some more interesting styles. There are thousands available on the Internet and on the cover-mounted CDs of computer and digital photography magazines. So, go browse!

A step further

When you've got a sizeable collection of pictures, you might consider getting a database program, both to organize and display your work. Look at the website of a huge commercial photographic agency (try *www.creative.gettyimages.com*) to see how they employ this type of software to help customers to search for pictures by "keywords," and eventually purchase images online. But let's take this one step at a time. An ordinary spreadsheet program can be surprisingly useful in displaying your images. We suggest some ideas on page 48 for creating an eye-catching, interactive calendar.

Digital cameras

SOFTWARE

DIGITAL CAMERAS

SCANNERS

THE INTERNET

PRINTERS

DIGITAL MEDIA

If you're a photo buff, you will already have information overload about the competing qualities of dozens of digital cameras. You may even have distilled this information enough to make a choice and part with your money. In which case, you'll know that however many millions of pixels of resolution there are in your new camera, it's already too few—overtaken by new models with more buttons and dials. If you're not a photo buff, you still need to have an idea what all this means, since resolution, pixels, and the rest are vital concepts in understanding how pictures arrive on paper or on the screen. Even if you don't plan to shoot digital pictures, you'll still need a grasp of the terms when it comes to manipulating your photos and getting them into shape for presentation. There's no way around it!

Do more dots mean better pictures?

In a normal film camera, light falls onto sensitive film. The processed image consists of millions of tiny, colored grains—so many, in fact, that the brain is fooled into thinking that the eyes see a continuous, smooth blend of color. In a digital camera, the film is replaced by a fixed sheet, which is electrically charged to be sensitive to light. The millions of

Left: This Olympus 35mm SLR (single-lens reflex) is just one example of a mid-range, non-digital, semi-automatic camera. The lens is excellent, and it includes a deep, motorized zoom.

Above: As digital cameras become more affordable, quality improves even at the "point and shoot" end of the market. This Olympus C-100 has a 1.3 Megapixel resolution— more than enough for Web usage.

film grains are replaced by millions of tiny squares, each one a receptor. Each of these millions of receptors records the color of light striking it. The information from all of these is gathered into a single, computer-readable file and stored temporarily in the camera.

So far, so straightforward, but are the pictures any good? Surely these receptors can't be as tiny and detailed as the grains in "proper" photographic film? The answer is to turn the question on its head, and ask "what do you want your pictures for?" Conventional color film can be used to make a 20" x 16" print with little or no perceptible grain structure to spoil the effect. Digital photos still have some way to go to match that level, but high-quality 8" x 10" prints are now commonplace. For normal album or website use, this is more than plenty. More receptors mean more detail. Large image files need storage, both in the camera's memory card and on your computer. So, be prepared to see your hard disk invaded by very large quantities of data—then we'll show you how to avoid being buried alive! But one thing is certain: digital photography means point, shoot, download: there's no wait.

The hard part:
the math of image and resolution

Your computer screen (working at 72 or 96 pixels per inch [ppi]) shows at least 800 pixels across by 600 pixels down: that's 480,000, nearly half a million pixels. But put your nose up to the screen and you can see the dots. Although it looks bright and cheerful, it would make a poor-quality print. Now imagine a typical camera with a two-million pixel (2Mp) capability. It can make a picture around 1632 pixels across by 1224 down. This would cover your screen four times over, or, more usefully, could be squeezed down, keeping all the pixels intact, to produce a postcard-size print of real quality.

To make that change, you would decrease the image size and increase the resolution. This is the heart of the matter: when the image gets to the moment of printing out, pixels get left behind. Image size is measured in the familiar units of inches (or millimeters for the Europeans), printer resolution is in dots per inch (dpi). The file size (the space the image occupies on your computer) may well remain the same. In our *Glossary* you can look up all these terms, and much more. "Headache" is the word for what you get trying to understand all this, but smugness is what you feel when you get the point!

The digital revolution among professional photographers and consumers alike has created a bewildering array of shapes, sizes, and models to choose from. Like the Olympus C-100, *opposite*, this Imax model also has a 1.3 Megapixel resolution. So, compare price and storage options (see page 22). Failing that, which would you like to be seen carrying on the beach?

Scanners

SOFTWARE

DIGITAL CAMERAS

▶ SCANNERS

THE INTERNET

PRINTERS

STORAGE MEDIA

Digital photography is a relatively new activity. Film- or plate-based photography dates from the middle of the 19th century, back when folks got a reputation for being stiff and unemotional because they had to stay still for the camera. So if you're lucky enough to have ancestors with a sense of history, you may possess pictures from over 150 years ago. Even for the majority of us not so blessed, there's still an extraordinary treasure trove of photographs, movies, objects, newspaper clippings, diaries, letters, postcards, certificates and diplomas, drawings, legal documents, books, and other evocative items waiting to be reborn. If you have no such history, concentrate on the present—and start one!

Slide, Charlie Brown, slide! Some scanners are designed, or have a transparency hood, for scanning transparent originals. So, if you have a lot of old faithfuls like these, or plan to shoot new ones, something like this might be a worthwhile investment. Then you can edit out that 1970s hair...

Acquiring the image

To get all these "legacy" images into usable form you need a scanner. Relentless competition among manufacturers has made a basic scanner less expensive than a reasonable meal for two. If you've just bought a computer, your supplier may well have bundled the scanner in for "free," and most scanners come with their own basic software.

Most of these simple scanners are "flatbed" designs, intended to deal with ordinary letter-size originals and smaller items. You lift the lid, place the image face-down on the glass plate, and set the relevant software going. Most times the scanning function will form part of an image-editing program. After the scanning lamp has passed quickly across the image area, your screen will show a preview window offering a low-resolution scan of the subject and the opportunity to set a number of controls (see *opposite* for a practical example). You might decide to scan part of the image, and "crop out" the rest.

The machine is set up to expose for the "average" original. Change the settings if necessary, hit *OK* and a slower

Never the Twain shall meet? Nonsense! Photoshop Elements and other bitmap image-editing packages give you the option of kick-starting your scanning package through the *Import* menu. In this way, you can import the image directly into your editing software... then it's over to you!

This handsome Umax scanner is typical of the flatbed type that you can buy separately at relatively low cost, or, with some makes, get bundled with new PCs. They come with their own software, or you can buy a more sophisticated scanning package if you wish, but it's almost certainly unnecessary. In any event, most scanning software operates in a similar way (see below). Simply place your original on the glass, close the lid, and fire up your software. Then after a few experimental passes, you can play around with the scanned image on your computer to your heart's content!

Scanning package Vistascan, *below*, offers some useful features. One is the ability to compensate for different types of original, such as newsprint. Newspapers and magazines can be a nightmare for scanners, as the dot screen used in the printing process and, in the case of newspapers, the "dot gain" of the ink on the absorbent paper, are difficult to read and to clean up. Vistascan allows you to "descreen" them. In practice, though, these procedures are often best carried out later in an image-editing program rather than "at source." But newspapers are just *so* last century, aren't they?

pass will produce an image at your chosen size and resolution. More expensive scanners might come with a "transparency hood" instead of a simple lid. This contains a second scanning unit, designed to acquire images by projecting light through a slide or transparency. The main difference is the greatly increased magnification required to get a reasonable result from a 35mm original, for example. But that also means dust and debris become, literally, a bigger problem, especially with old originals, so a can of compressed air is a vital accessory to clean the images.

If you have many transparencies to deal with, then consider purchasing a dedicated film scanner. Results from these more costly machines are usually much better, especially in capturing the dynamic range of transparency film, but if you are determined never to shoot transparency film again, rent or borrow one for a while and patiently scan the cream of your collection for future use.

Size and resolution

Even a simple flatbed scanner will offer a huge ratio of enlargement (or reduction). The initial temptation to scan everything at high resolution (say 600 dots per inch) and at 300% enlargement will soon subside at the sight of the resulting file sizes filling up your computer. And there is no point scanning an old, out-of-focus photo at high resolution; all you'll get is a big, soft mess. Try instead to predict the eventual size you'll need, then set the controls accordingly.

The Internet

The best parts of the Internet comprise a marvelous resource when looking for inspiration in designing and organizing your photo scrapbook. The worst might turn your hair gray, if it isn't already. You can look at everything from tin toy collecting sites, online auction services, and archives of rare postcards, to websites created at enormous cost by corporations selling everything from tequila to toothbrushes. Look, admire, and, most of all, borrow their ideas. Alternatively, feel much better about your own creative abilities once you've laughed at the competition.

Getting connected

Skip this if you're already online. You'll need a modem (standard fitting inside most recent computers, but also available as an accessory), a phone line, and the telephone number of an ISP (Internet Service Provider). Your computer

may already contain one or more ISPs' details, and also the necessary "browser" software to navigate the Internet. Alternatively, pick up a cover-mounted CD from a magazine (hey, remember to buy the magazine first!). It should contain all you need to connect to a particular provider. Best of all, ask an experienced friend for a recommendation. The connection process can be frustrating—rather like the terms freely used by those in the know: HTTP, FTP, DNS, and the rest. See our Glossary for all these acronyms and more. Your connection to a service provider should get you onto the Internet and provide you with an email address. There may be costs; at least in the US, the actual call charges are free.

What's it for?

The Internet is the world's biggest library, so how do you find all this stuff on its virtual shelves without knowing where to look? Well, the Internet is patrolled by robots. But these aren't the tin men of science fiction, but pieces of intelligent software that search the entire interconnected network (Internet) for documents and websites that match the words or terms you've requested.

Your browser will probably direct you to a home page, such as MSN (Microsoft's network), or AOL, from which you can search with varying degrees of success, as well as find a variety of new content every day. Be wary, however, of some commercial "portals": they exist to sell you products and services and to direct you to other content owned by that company. Fortunately, there are dozens of specialist "search

Google (*www.google.com*) is one of the best search engines—you can use it to find pictures and newsgroups too, and even filter out "adult" content.

We've done a picture search and a general search for "family tree." Google turned up 7,500 images in less than a quarter of a second, and more than 750,000 related websites in a quarter of that time! If you refine the search using your own family name, you might dig up some ancestors...

engine" websites out there. Think of them as your intelligent and endlessly patient librarians. In reality, a search engine is a powerful array of computers that stores and organizes billions of references, and is accessed by one of those "software robots" that search for matching references. Many are fast and excellent, and will actually retrieve documents that match what you're looking for.

Try calling up a search engine, such as Google at *www.google.com*, and enter a single chosen word. Let's say you were looking for references to "carolina" (capital letters are ignored by the search engine). Google will respond in well under a second with perhaps 12,600,000 webpages (or "hits" in the jargon). If you search for the same term in a year's time, that figure will probably be much higher, as more and more sites are added to the Internet. Obviously it pays to be more specific! Try again with "south carolina" and you get just over three million hits—better, but still far too much reading. "south carolina ancestors" yields a mere 142,000. Inserting a half-remembered first name gets you nearly down

to the wire: "giuseppe south carolina ancestors" produces only 241 responses. Interestingly, misspelling "giuseppe" as "guiseppe" still gets you 76 hits, and a helpful query from Google: "did you mean giuseppe?"

As well as letting you admire other sites, the Internet plugs you into a worldwide community of special-interest groups. If you need help in constructing a family tree, there's a legion of people who know all about genealogy, even heraldry; when you're struggling to restore an old photograph on screen, you'll find tutorial pages from the software developer or from groups of enthusiasts; if you'd like to see what the newspapers said the day your grandfather was born, there's a good chance that an old archive will display that golden day.

Some sites can even learn your preferences, or let you search for pictures, video clips, people, or pieces of music. They will dig up millions of online communities of hobbyists, collectors, writers, photographers, experts... and you should be able to find what you're looking for. And if you join one or many of these communities, you'll quickly find yourself part of a global network of people who share your passions and enthusiasms—and quite a few who don't!

If you want to search for a phrase like "family tree," rather than the two words separately, type the phrase in double quotes as we've just done. More on family trees later.

Printers

Finally comes the time to print out your picture, and the aim is the preservation of all the quality that was recorded by the camera or scanner—perhaps with your contribution of retouching and adjustment. The computer monitor shows a bright, saturated image made of tiny glowing red, green, and blue phosphors, and it may take a while to accept that no combination of printer and paper is ever going to reproduce that brilliance. The monitor is a remarkable piece of engineering, but there is more rocket science in the typical inkjet color printer. Your picture file is reproduced as microscopic dots of cyan (light blue), magenta (a vivid purple), yellow, and black. With a magnifying lens you'll see exactly the same colors making up the color images in this book, but there is a crucial difference. There are around 150

One of the by-products of digital technology becoming smaller, faster, and less expensive with each new generation has been that computers and their peripheral devices, like printers, have become simpler and more attractive to look at. In the wake of Apple's iMac, PC hardware has jumped on the design bandwagon. This simple Compaq desktop printer is still not the most attractive color in the world, but at least it won't clutter your desk.

Color printing technology ranges from the quiet desktop inkjet, like this neat and low-cost Epson (*right*), to larger professional devices that can turn out poster-sized originals, like this Kodak (*below*). But stick with the former... unless your ambition gets the better of you.

dots per inch on this page, but up to 2400 per inch in a photo-quality inkjet print, each one squirted at the right place on the paper by heat or vibration. The print head stops momentarily to fire four dots at a time, but the process is so rapid that it looks like continuous motion.

Going dotty for pixels?

Remember always that these dots are not the same as pixels. If you try to increase your image resolution to 2400 pixels per inch, your computer will be swamped with enormous files, and you'll spend hours waiting for prints with no extra quality. The printer software (the "driver") works best when interpreting your 300 pixel per inch file, approximating colors where they blend into each other and smoothing rough edges. Each printer manufacturer has a proprietary method for enhancing your images. If you don't approve, you can sometimes switch it off and make your own settings. At the more expensive end of the market you'll find completely different printers: dye-sublimation; thermal wax; thermal autochrome (where the color is already in the paper and is activated by heat); and four-color versions of the regular laser printer. But remember: it's results that really count.

Paper

Inkjet printers demand special papers. Although you can use ordinary copier paper for test prints—there's normally a setting to reduce ink flow—you'll produce a mess if you use it for finished work. There are high-gloss coated papers, silk and matt finish, heavyweight cardboard, decal papers for decorating sweatshirts and ceramics, long rolls for banners and panoramas, and canvas-textured paper for an "antique" result. As long as your ink holds out, the possibilities are endless. And speaking of ink... low-budget printers have small ink cartridges containing all four colors, or three colors with a separate black. The small capacity, and high relative cost, of these cartridges is a major source of frustration for anyone attempting to produce photo-quality prints. If you can, choose a printer with separate, large-capacity tanks for each color. Keep a reserve stock, one of each color, and use the printer's built-in software to check the levels in the printer. Your black cartridge will probably run dry first.

Saving to digital media

We've already looked at the business of saving pictures on your own hard disk, but there are two other crucial storage issues to discuss. First, and infinitely most important, is the question of backing up. Imagine this sequence of events: you shoot lots of pictures and the camera's built-in storage or memory card fills up. To free up space, you transfer the pictures to your computer, work on them, and integrate them into an album or project. Then you have second thoughts about your first attempts and start to remake the adjustments on copies of your original shots, or maybe decide to put the whole thing on the back burner for later, although your family would like to see prints of the pictures right now. This is an excellent recipe for disaster. Only when your hard disk has expired without trace, or someone has walked away with your computer will you become a true believer in backup.

Media types

Let's begin with the simplest device, the floppy disk, and dismiss it completely: it doesn't hold much information and it's far too slow. Many new computers don't include a floppy drive anymore. Realistic solutions start with the CD-ROM (Compact Disc Read-Only Memory), and recent computers allow you to record a CD right in the slot where you normally read them. You could also buy an external CD writer. The storage available on a standard CD is up to 700 Mb—room for up to 100 letter-sized pictures saved as JPEG files at 300 dpi (see page 44 for more on file-saving types). CDs are now an affordable and reliable medium, and they're easy to store and catalogue. You can also use just part of a disk, and fill the rest up at another "session." The negative side is the fairly slow copying process and the fact that, once used, the CD cannot be erased and reused. CD-RW (Rewriteable) overcomes that objection to the regular CD format, but there

Left: Clik disks are smaller than the Zip system (this is near actual size), and offer extreme portability. They're so small that you can buy a neat Clik disk reader for your laptop, no bigger than a credit card, and slot the disk into it. Useful for those secret missions! The Jaz, on the other hand, is the Clik's big brother, with 4Gb of capacity. Right: This Compact Flash card slots right into a Nikon digital camera, offering 8Mb of space. Below: IBM's Microdrive cards work on a similar principle.

is a doubt about the permanence of data recorded on this type of disk. DVD (Digital Video—or Versatile—Disk) is discussed both as a creative and storage medium later in this book (see page 90). As an alternative, think of other disk-based systems such as Zip, with capacities of up to 250 Mb, or of removable hard drives. There are many models in the market, and transfer speed and capacity increase all the time. On the plus side of the latter is the enormous hike in capacity to a typical 40 Gb. That's around 60 times more than a regular CD, and connection methods like FireWire make for fast transfer. The drives themselves are small—pocketable in fact. But there is the ever-present, though remote, fear of eventual mechanical failure. Taking the long view, it is expected that the data on regular CDs will have a useful life of up to 100 years when properly stored. To be extra sure, store long-term on brand-name CDs, and also print out on good-quality paper and let posterity take care of itself…

Far left and top left: Iomega's Zip Drive system is just one of several, portable, high-capacity storage products made by the company. Zip disks are robust (contained within a cartridge-like shell), and have capacities of up to 250Mb. Left: A standalone high-speed CD rewriteable drive, which shows the influence of Apple's iMac. Right: A DVD / CD-RW (CD rewriteable) drive. Over the next two years, DVD writers will become less expensive and more commonplace.

Your home page

Despite the vast and ever-increasing extent of the Internet, there are millions of Megabytes of unused webspace whirling around on Web servers worldwide. Almost everyone who ever signed up for an Internet connection received, as part of the deal, a patch of virgin territory (usually around 20 Mb of webspace). This might sound meager given the huge amounts of file storage discussed on earlier pages, but it's more than enough real estate on which to cultivate a flourishing home page. Wagonloads of visitors are sure to pass by, appreciating your fine crops of images and finely wrought text. So, fired up with pioneering spirit, where's the beef?

Looking for content—and an audience

For many, the technical challenge of setting up a website is pleasure enough. The result on screen might be pedestrian,

but at least it's there. But the decision about what to display is the hardest of all. Be jealous of the woman with the world's second largest collection of miniature whiskey bottles. She already has content, images in the making, structure, and, probably, an audience. Be very jealous of the guy with two hundred schemes for reducing your income tax bill. He has compulsive text, step-by-step examples and, potentially, a lucrative enterprise (although thousands of failed commercial ventures had the same belief). If you resemble neither of these characters, then you should start with a more readily available subject: your family, your work, your hobbies, or your collections, for example. Alternatively, you could research your ancestry and consider building an interactive family tree—we'll cover all this and more in our projects.

But who will see your site? Assuming you have some text on your site, the search engines (see page 19) will eventually find you. You can speed up the process by registering your site with some of the major search engines, but you won't find yourself coming up on a search immediately. So be patient. Equally, there are many awards handed out for new, well-designed, and content-rich sites. Although the awards generally bring only prestige, rather than cash, at least your site could be promoted on the grapevine. Such is the multiplication factor of anything placed on the Internet. Your exposure will be worldwide before you know it. If you want it to be, that is.

Setting your sights

Start with pen and paper. Draw four small boxes in a line and imagine what you'd like to see in each. The first one inevitably becomes a kind of title page and leads on to page two. That's where the similarity to a book ends abruptly. There's absolutely

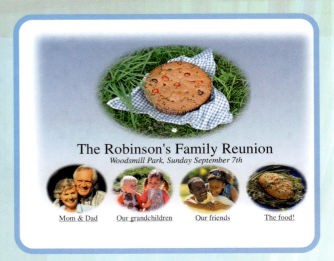

In a few pages' time you'll be able to build a website like this...

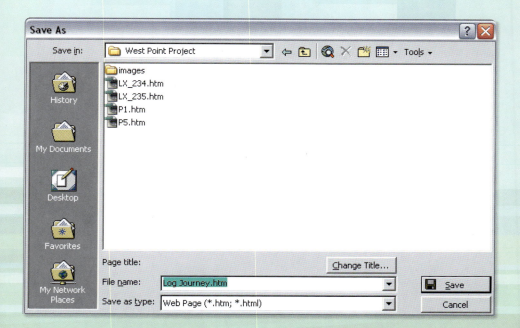

If you have a recent version of Microsoft Word installed (as part of the Microsoft Office package, for example) you'll find that you can turn a basic wordprocessor document into a simple webpage. Not all of the functions work when saving a Word document into HTML, but you can design a perfectly acceptable page this way. There'll be more on this in the projects ahead. But once you've finished preparing your document, just select *Save as Web Page* from the file menu (or *Save as HTML*, depending on the version).

no reason why page three should follow two. You can give viewers the choice of jumping straight to page four if the prospect of page three doesn't thrill them. Pretty soon you'll have seven pages, with arrows linking them in a tangle of lines. This is by far the best stage to make decisions about scope and content, long before concerning yourself with image size, resolution, and the overall design of your home on the Web (again, see the projects to find out more). Aim for six pages or fewer as a first attempt—it's very easy to add more as you develop the site further. That's the beauty of the Web.

A thought for the user

This is also a good time to consider the eventual viewer of your site. If you already use the Internet to any extent you will have already experienced the tedium of waiting ages for a webpage to download, or of long scrolling pages filled with repetitive text. Then there's the frustration of finding no way back to the home page due to the absence of links, or links that just don't work. Try to resolve these issues at the outset by estimating the number of words on a typical page, and establishing relevant links between sections—all still with pen and paper. It may look rough, but it will save all kinds of pain later. For you and for your visitors.

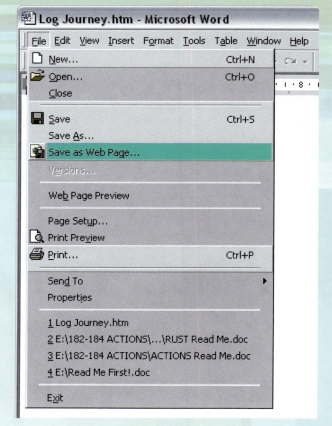

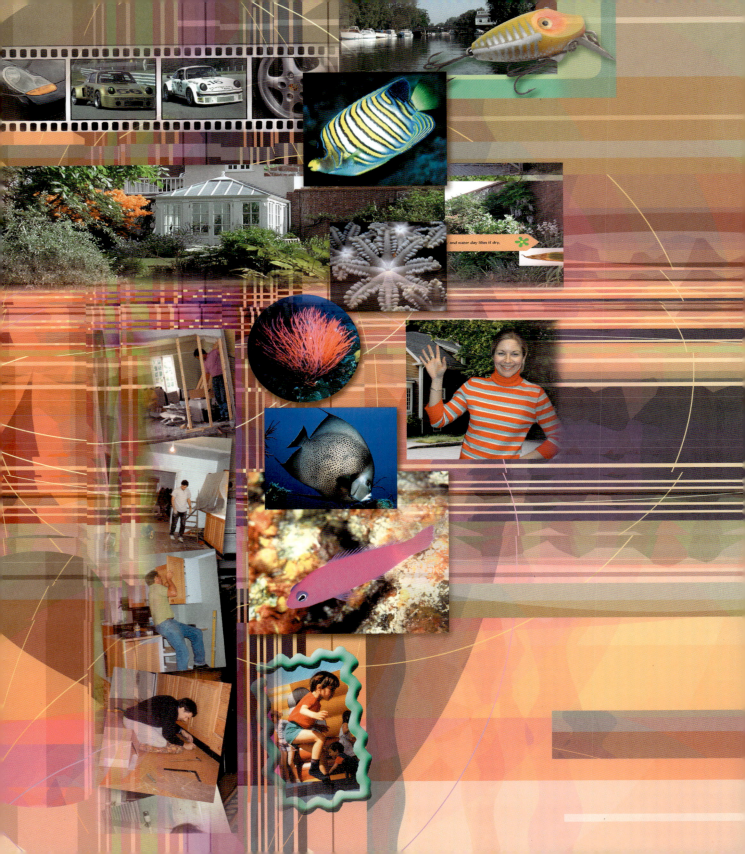

The Projects

OK, we've done the science bit! Now all you need is to get your imagination fired up, boot up your computer, make yourself comfortable, and try out these easy-to-follow, fun projects that will give your memories a whole new lease of life. Let's turn your scissors and paste scrapbook into an interactive experience for you, your family, and friends to enjoy, wherever in the world they might be...

BEFORE YOU START...
- Not all of the equipment below is absolutely essential, but to get the most out of the projects in this book, you will need:
- A Windows PC (Windows 95 up to Windows XP), or an Apple Macintosh (such as an iMac) running Mac OS 9 or OS X. A good wordprocessing program, such as Microsoft Word, would be an advantage. If you have the full Microsoft Office suite, then so much the better... and a CD drive would really put you ahead of the game.
- A digital camera, or a good-quality conventional camera and an image scanner. If you've got a video camera, especially a digital one, then you'll get the most out of the later projects.
- A basic image-editing program, such as Adobe Photoshop Elements or similar (we'll tell you the options).
- A basic website-building program, such as HotDog, Composer, or similar (we'll tell you what to do if you don't have this).
- Loads of imagination, some ideas, and all the old photos, memorabilia, souvenirs, and mementoes you can find!
- Oh... and that Internet connection! Got it all? Here we go...

A vacation album

Let's dive straight into a rich photo resource. What's the best vacation you've ever had? Where are the pictures? Let's hope you didn't forget your camera—and that you know where your old-style album is! Your collection, whether it's carefully organized with every picture captioned and dated, or stacked in an old grocery box, is a priceless treasury of memories. In this project we'll give you the key to unlock it; to transform these ready-made images into a new experience, an album that will delight its viewers all over again. This first project is about giving you an insight into the qualities of a good picture. Why is it that some images tell a story while others stare dumbly back at you? How come some pictures work well in combination, while others need to be strictly on their own?

Many billions of photographs have been taken since the invention of photography by the Frenchman Nicéphore Niepcé. Or was it William Fox Talbot, as the English insist? What's certain is that Fox Talbot was spurred into action by a vacation experience. His companions were all accomplished artists, recording everything in sketchbooks, while he could only look through the lens of a camera obscura and attempt to trace around what he saw. Some 150 years later his and Niepcé's technology allows all of us to capture the moment without effort.

Beached!
This one has it all. Surprise, humor, good composition, varied texture, harmonious color, creative viewpoint. If you have even a few pictures like this, your project will be a snap.

THE IMPORTANCE OF VIEWPOINT

Most conventional cameras sit naturally in the hands with the shutter button under the right forefinger, the right eye looking through the viewfinder and the left hand adjusting focus. That's why the great majority of photographs end up in landscape format, shot from eye level. This can be great—but it can also be boring. It's natural to want to include as much as possible in every shot, but the result can be a picture with no point of emphasis. A show without a star.

The plain vanilla shot: there's plenty of detail but nothing leaps out to grab you. Put this one in the "back in the basement" pile.

The chocolate-chip shot: getting in close, or zooming if you're nervous, produces a far more exciting image.

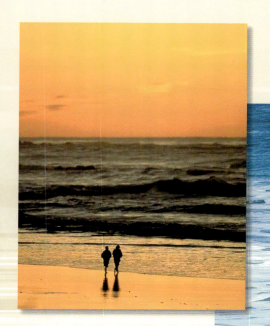

Warm Horizons
A good example of when to let nature take its course: the faraway shot that works. Bold stripes of color and a strong sense of scale, all wrapped in spectacular evening light.

Back to the Future
Forget the old instruction books: There are moments when the back view is best. You can almost feel the waves around your toes, inviting you to join the rush to the sea. But have these guys got cold feet?

Close Up and Personal
Is this the yard of beach next to your foot, or an aerial shot of strange mountain ranges? This miniature landscape has much of the fascination of the full-size version. You can use details like this creatively, as we'll explore later...

If you don't yet own a digital camera, consider investing in one: prices are falling, and you'll find it easy to gather and store thousands of images for posterity. If you own one already, you may have a collection of vacation pictures that cry out to be displayed to their best advantage. But if you are still in the foothills of making that decision, your raw materials for now will be your existing prints, slides—perhaps even movie or video footage (see page 76 for ways to get results out of the moving image).

As well as conventional images like these, you can use all the other bits and pieces that you've probably saved to remind you of that special time. Look for postcards, theater programs, travel tickets, and tags. See over the page for an example of how you can add these items to your digital photo scrapbook, and turn your ephemera into something more permanent. This project aims to reassemble a number of existing album pictures and print them out as complete sheets. There are several practical considerations that may influence the choice of images from an existing album. Very old pictures stored in unfavorable conditions can suffer from blemishes of various kinds. Some of the problems your old pictures might have are: mold; discoloration due to glue staining through the back of the print; damage on the front through being stuck to other prints or to the album leaves themselves; fading of the image due to sun exposure or insufficient chemical fixing when first made; brown staining from iron oxide in the album or the print substrate; all the way through to scribbling marks made by disrespectful relatives. All these faults can be cured, or at least improved, using the digital techniques outlined in Project Six, and on pages 142 and 143.

Transferring from a digital camera
If your camera contains a removable memory device like a CompactFlash, SmartMedia, or MemoryStick storage card, you can insert the card into a reader, which then plugs into a port (usually the USB slot) on your computer, and download the pictures to your hard disk. There is often a cable alternative linking the camera and computer directly. If the camera only has a fixed internal memory, you'll need to use the cable method.

Just place the print on the scanner, then rev up your software engines...

Scanning existing pictures
Very good results can be obtained using an ordinary desktop scanner. In fact, you will often be able to improve the appearance of old pictures with just a few adjustments, either in the scanner's own software, or afterwards in an image-editing program.

You can store dozens of images on any of the memory cards or sticks that come with some digital still and video cameras. Then just slot into the reader and... you're off.

Ah, springtime in Paris. With a quick fix in Vistascan, this is sharper, more colorful, and better all round.

Those of you who have never stolen hotel soap should skip over these pages. In this project, you can use your vacation "ephemera" such as travel tickets, souvenir bookmarks, shades, keyfobs, and guidebooks to complement your photographs. Your scanner can deal with shallow, three-dimensional objects, although you shouldn't chance your scanner's glass surface with large chunks of Ayers Rock or the Grand Canyon. On the other hand, items like that can make handy targets for close-up photography with your digital (or conventional) camera to give your scrapbook a real sense of place. The more you travel the world, the more you'll see that local graphic designs and typography reflect the countries and cities you visit: the chic lettering on the shopping bags from your trip down the Champs Élysées, for example; the bright, sunny colors from your West Coast beach vacation...

To further blur the edges between your photos and the local culture of your vacation destination, why not try inserting one into the other? Scan the front page of the local newspaper you picked up and use an image-editing program to add your family members, and revise the headlines to announce your arrival in town. The techniques to do this are basically the same as the retouching tricks you need to work on faulty pictures (which we'll deal with throughout the book).

Look at the size of the items at your disposal and enlarge or reduce them dramatically. For example, you can use the airline tag from your suitcase as an all-over background for a whole album page. Make a pattern out of those left-over banknotes, coins, and unspent traveler's checks. The door is open wide for the enthusiastic scanner operator!

Above: **Clean Up!**
If there are specks of dust on your scan or on your original, or if the original picture has been damaged in some way, you can use some of the repair tools and filters in Photoshop Elements to fix them. *Dust & Scratches*; *Restore Damaged Photo; Red Eye* and *Quick Fix* (for contrast and so on) are just some of the options.

Ayers on a Shoestring
Small objects can be scanned and turned into a digital image you can use like any other, or a background texture for a page.

Colorizing Monochrome Graphics
Maybe your album page is a little light on colorful items. It's easy to change dull bits of newsprint, for example, into brilliantly colored gems. All that's needed is some contrast between the tones in the original. Select one shade of gray in an image-editing program, and fill it with vermilion, select another gray and fill with turquoise. With digital techniques, the options are limitless.

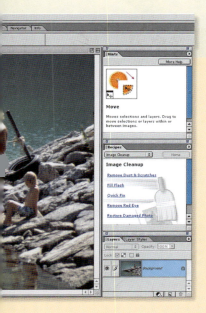

Right: There are two routes to producing a complex collage like this. Route One has you arranging your items in perfect order on the scanner, taking care to overlap each one and, much more difficult than it might seem, getting them absolutely at right angles relative to the edges of the scanner glass. Assuming you can keep things organized (and remember, your images need to be face down, not face up!), it's just one scan and you're done. Route 2, though longer, is recommended. Put two or three items together on the glass, close but not touching, and scan them as a group or, if your scanner/ software combination will allow, as separate items. Separate scans will allow you to change the size of each item, giving you much more flexibility when assembling the collage. Following this method, you can assemble the scans layer by layer in your image-editing program, retouch them individually as required, and add shadows for that final, lifelike look.

Now for the easy bit. The pictures have been downloaded or scanned, sized, cropped, retouched, and stand ready for your final layout. With your computer, you have more than enough flexibility to change their relative sizes; but remember that scanned photos can always be quickly rescanned if they run out of definition under extreme enlargement. This is the moment to try any combination of pictures that appeals to your eye. You can try formal and informal layouts; you can overlap or not overlap; use vignettes and shadows. Liberated from the usual album constraints of glue pot, sticky corners, and rectangular picture shapes of fixed size and format, you are free to decide, change your mind, then decide again. You have all the possibilities of the newsstand magazine designer, with none of the deadlines. Take your time to swap the layers around. Keep back the picture that doesn't quite work, and store it for use in another layout. You'll begin to make judgments about what works well, and what doesn't. Developing this kind of selection process is vital groundwork for moving onto webpages and even more complex presentations. And we'll get onto those soon enough!

CHOOSING PAPER

Glossy papers offer the most saturated colors, although the complexity of the coatings makes them comparatively expensive. Unfortunately, a deal of trial and error is necessary before you find a brand that suits your eye, and your pocket. Some cheaper papers skimp on the coating process; the worst offenders will show ugly bands of varying density. Your printer software will usually offer different settings for various kinds of paper, and adjust the ink flow automatically to get the best result. At the top end of the market, you'll find inkjet-suitable "watercolor" papers, which actually come from the same mills where the regular artists' version is produced. Other unusual surfaces include imitation silk on a plastic sheet.

Resolution

Above: Your printer probably offers "draft" quality for speed and economy. The number of dots of ink is reduced and the print-head moves rapidly across the paper surface. The trade-off may sometimes be acceptable, but most times you'll want to stick to high resolution for printed work.

Playing it Straight

The traditional rectangular layout (*above left*) needs strong images like this to keep the eye interested. A small vignette provides good contrast.

The Layered Effect

Angled pictures must be handled with care. Borders and backgrounds help make both these sets of images work together, giving a real sense of place to bring back those precious memories.

Now that you have your pictures selected, enhanced where necessary, and composited into single sheets with vignettes, drop shadows, applied textures, and scanned memorabilia, it's a good time to consider the final format and style of your newly revamped, conventional scrapbook. If you buy a commercial product, these decisions are mostly made for you. Depending on your budget you can choose padded covers, gold blocking, elaborate interleaving, even an integral musical box (if that's to your taste). In theory you could use any kind of blank book.

If you're a practical person, it's not hard to construct an album of your own. Imagine you have some stunning panorama shots. It's a crime to stick them across two pages with a gap in the middle. Why not mount your panoramas back-to-back on thin cardboard? Then make matching front and back covers on heavier cardboard, and get the local print or copy shop to bind the whole production together. They can generally offer plastic comb binding (not very beautiful, but effective and strong), Wire-O (more elegant, and more expensive), or, if you only have a few prints, a simple slide-on plastic spine. If you prefer to do the whole job yourself, be careful with that Scotch tape: your efforts will look a whole lot better after 20 years without a garland of semiliquid gloop.

TELLING THE TALE OF YOUR VACATION

The secret of this first, easy project—and of digital scrapbooking techniques in general—is to choose, edit, and compile images that really tell the story of your vacation. So, page one could be leaving home, the trip to the airport, the baggage—and the inevitable wait. Move onto page two and you've arrived exhausted at your destination, probably hours late and yearning for the comfort of your hotel room. Keep the tickets if you can, the menu at the hotel, a napkin or two, maybe even that vital '"Do Not Disturb" sign in six languages. All will take on a life of their own once you've scanned them, edited and composited them in your image-editing program. Then it's straight onto the main event: those days on the beach; the local bars and restaurants; the guide books and souvenirs; those few secretly taken snapshots of family members as they complained about the service. It's your story!

Preserving your Work

Once you've composed a few pages of pictures, put your drop shadows in place, and maybe scanned some textures or found objects, it's time to start compiling your new, improved, yet still-traditional album. Why not try canvas-textured paper for an economical "fine-art" look. Or make two moves in your image-editing program: use the *Watercolor* function to give a painterly effect over the whole layout, then choose *Canvas Texture* as an overall filter.

Lickety-stick

Who remembers lick-and-stick photo corners? The modern way is to protect the prints under a thin transparent sheet. As a bonus, static electricity holds them firmly in position. Avoid albums with actively adhesive sheets of any kind—every bit of lint you ever saw will be preserved forever.

The family event @ home page

Take your place on the worldwide stage with this fun-to-do family Web project. Whether you delve into your store of existing images or set up a whole new event just to be sure of getting the shots you want, creating this kind of record is an ideal way of honing your picture-making skills. You select the shots, you direct the layout, you mastermind the order of events—and with our help you can overcome the technical challenges of assembling your first scrapbook and uploading it to the Internet. It's easy!

Digital technology can help you bring your family pictures to life on the Internet, and that's what we're going to do with this project. But first, there's some more technical stuff to get through before we move deeper into the projects...

We've looked at the basic technical issues surrounding websites in our introduction. But what about the software? If you wanted to, you could learn HTML, but these days there is no need to do this: a whole host of programs will write the code for you "behind the scenes," and you need never know what it looks like, or what it does. But if you're keen to find out, the big screen of code *opposite* is what HTML is really like.

If you have Microsoft Office installed, many of the programs in the suite have a *Save as HTML* function. Take Word, for example. You can turn just about any document prepared in Word, which might include photos and graphics, into an HTML document (your own webpage) and publish it on the Internet, burn it onto a CD, or email it to your friends. It's easy! There are dozens of other options, but let's talk Word first.

The Secret Code

Lurking behind every webpage is a secret code, called HTML, which describes how each element of a page appears (and tells your browser where to find other elements, like graphics or sound files). Here it is... ugh!

```
<HTML>

<HEAD>
<META NAME="keywords" CONTENT="macint
<META NAME="description" CONTENT="Ma

<TITLE>MacAddict 10.1</TITLE>
</HEAD>
<script language="javascript">mpt = new
<script language="javascript" src="/ads

<body bgcolor="#66FF66" marginwidth="0"

<table width=98% border=0 cellpadding=0
<tr>
   <td align=center width="100%" cols
<img src="images/logo_home.gif" wid
<script language="JavaScript">
<!-- Hide from old browsers
document.write('<a href="' + Bimglink
// -- End Hiding Here -->
</script>
</td>
</tr>

<tr>
<td bgcolor="ffffff" rowspan=2 width=42
   <noscript><img src="/images/nav.gif"
<td bgcolor="66ff66" width="66%" valign
<img src="/images/blank.gif" width=2 he
</td>
</tr>
<tr>
<td bgcolor="ffffff" width="66%" valign
<!----------------SEARCH LINK---------
<table border="0" cellpadding="3" cells
   <tr>
   <td align="right" valign="middle" w
<!-- Atomz Search HTML for MacAddict Se
<form name="seek" method="get" action="
<input type=hidden name="sp-a" value="s
<input type=submit name="go" value="Go!
<input type="text" name="sp-q" size="19
</form>
   </td>
      </tr>
   </table>
<br clear=all>
   <table border=0 cellpadding=0 cells
   <tr>
   <td bgcolor="#003366" align=center
```

Title: MacAddict 10.1

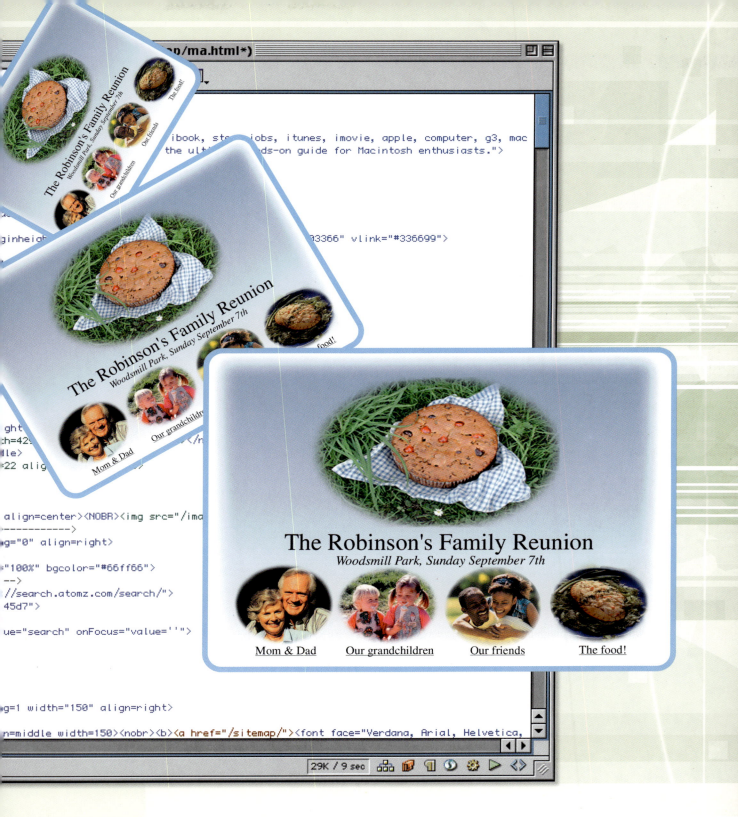

The Robinson's Family Reunion
Woodsmill Park, Sunday September 7th

Mom & Dad   Our grandchildren   Our friends   The food!

Once you've produced a page in Word, simply select *Save as HTML* from the *File* menu. You can then open this document in your Web browser (you probably have Explorer or Navigator, but any one, such as Opera *www.opera.com* is as good, if not better). Of course, the document still sits on your computer—it's not yet on the Internet. We'll show you how to post it online in a few pages' time.

If you want to see what the HTML version of your document looks like for yourself, simply select *Source* in Explorer, or *View Source* in Navigator, and you will see a screen full of HTML that the program has written for you behind the scenes.

Using this technique (in Word you'll also need to select *Online Layout* from the *View* menu) you can quickly transform simple documents into effective webpages, but some of the familiar Word features can't be used. The multicolumn "newspaper" style layout, for example, doesn't transfer across, but there are plus points as well. You can select a range of a background colors and patterns that aren't available in the wordprocessor version.

But as you grow more confident, you'll quickly tire of such beginner-level functions. If you want complete freedom when laying out text and pictures, there are dedicated programs available such as Dreamweaver, HomeSite (it's cheap, but you'll need to learn HTML!), GoLive, and HotDog (an excellent starter). They are used by many professional webpage producers to make commercial sites, and are therefore loaded with features you'll never need, and maneuvers you'll be glad you never had to learn. But they are fun to use at the basic level. You can also pick up free or trial packages on magazines' cover-mounted free CDs. The Netscape Web browser offers a built-in program called "Composer," with which you can build simple websites. If it's not installed on your computer, download it from *www.netscape.com*, or pick up a free CD.

Alternatively, get a free trial of Moonfruit at *www.moonfruit.com*. This is an online service that allows you to build fun, professional-looking websites in a couple of hours over the Internet, without buying any software. There's no HTML to learn, and there are tutorials to help you along. Your page won't turn up on search engines, but you can still send your friends the Web address. Now, let's turn your family event into a fun, interactive scrapbook that will give your photos a new lease of life!

You've Seen How the Experts Do It...

You've watched Google search for webpages, pictures... even route you to websites that let you track down long-lost friends. But why not make your own webpage, or website, that brings those friends to you?

Back   Forward   Stop   Refresh   Home   AutoFill   Print   Mail

Address: @ http://images.google.com/images?hl=en&q=%22Friends+Reunited%22&btnG=Google+Search   go

@ Live Home Page   @ Apple   @ Apple Support   @ Apple Store   @ iTools   @ Mac OS X   @ Microsoft MacTopia   @ Office for Macintosh   @ MSN   @ Google

Google™

Advanced Image Search   Image Search Help

"Friends Reunited"   Google Search

Mature content filter is On

roups | Directory

iends Reunited".   Results **1 - 20** of about **72**. Search took **0.47** seconds.

fr-memory-top.gif
500 x 20 pixels - 1k
www.friendsreunited.co.uk/
[More results from
co.uk/   www.friendsreunited.co.uk]

side1.gif
180 x 169 pixels - 3k
www.happygroup.co.uk/

fr-heading.gif
500 x 20 pixels - 1k
www.happygroup.co.uk/
[More results from
www.happygroup.co.uk]

spotlight_mizulo1.jpg
150 x 224 pixels - 4k
www.activeshare.com/ US/dig/

viet_fam.JPG
240 x 160 pixels - 10k
www.redcross.org/news/in/

paul williams
paul-williams-title.gif
300 x 75 pixels - 2k
celigne.co.uk/paul/

farsons2.jpg
347 x 505 pixels - 24k
ourworld.compuserve.com/
homepages/ timjd/farsons.htm

41

Don't say a word! If your intended subjects—family, friends, or colleagues—suspect that they are about to become raw material for your Web project, you may well get an icy reaction. Although there are few people who still believe that the camera can steal the soul, you'll find many get ornery when being stage-managed. What you need is that most difficult combination: organized spontaneity. Dilute your presence as camera-person by inviting a crowd, setting up games and distractions, even getting a friend to act as a decoy photographer while you skulk around the edges of the event catching people off guard. Clearly, none of the above subterfuge is necessary if most of your subjects are natural actors, craving the adoring gaze of the camera.

To establish the sequence, try to get a really wide shot of the scene. The ideal one is before the fun starts (the calm before the storm?), making a handy contrast to the shot of everyone departing at the end. Shoot the invitation if there is one. Or if you made it on the computer, see if you can make a screen grab (see your computer operating system's instruction book). When things get started, you'll have to rely on your natural cunning to get the best shots, but there are a few tips to remember. Try to shoot everyone, since, in spite of their denials, no one likes to be left out. Get someone to shoot you, for the same reason. Shoot people doing something, even if it's only gesturing impatiently at you. Shoot from above; lie down and get a shot from the ground; shoot through trees, through windows and doors; shoot against the light; shoot the food and drink, and the kids at play; capture the adults in deep conversation, and don't forget the pets (they'll be far less self-conscious).

If you're shooting digitally and you're absolutely sure that these pictures will only be used on your Web project, set the camera to "basic" quality. This will normally give images of average screen size at 72 dots per inch, perfectly adequate for the Internet, allowing you many more shots—as well as longer battery life.

Getting Down to It
You'll be lucky to get a shot like this. Corn cobs and skewers rarely line up so neatly, and it's hard to get the people to do the same. Try, but don't get sunburned or sizzled by the barbecue.

Where's the Sun?
Try to break the old rule about having the sun immediately behind you. Faces look better when not in full sun. Eyes don't pucker up. And sometimes you get a bonus of a backlit halo of hair or a hat. Ah... a star is born.

Get in Close

Make it a priority to get some good food shots. And get in before the ketchup starts to fly!

The Aaah Factor

If you find this type of picture too sentimental for your project, maybe it will still work as your Christmas card, or as a calendar picture (see page 52).

Action is Everything

Lots of light, quick thinking, and a fast shutter speed gets you the reward. If you're using a digital camera, you can check the screen immediately to see if you hit the spot. If not, they might do it all over again. Some medical authorities reckon that holding children this way, though fun, is a bad idea.

Back at home in the calm glow of your monitor, it's time to review your harvest of pictures. If you've shot on conventional film, this selection procedure is especially important. There's no point in scanning stacks of prints that you know in your bones are never going to make it. If you've been shooting digitally, there's still a selection to be made. If you can't face the idea of trashing anything, then burn a CD (see page 90), or make some other form of backup. That way you can have the luxury of changing your mind right through the process.

In either case, you may find it useful to sort the pictures into groups onscreen. You could make folders called simply "start," "middle," and "end," for example. Soon you'll have another folder called "odd," and another one called "email" containing pictures so hilarious that they won't wait to be turned into a webpage, but have to be emailed *right now*.

LOSE THAT WEIGHT / WAIT

Welcome to the hard realities of image compression. The same law that makes your digital camera run snappily on the *Basic* setting means that Web pictures have to be slimmed down as well. There are several ways this can be done. Your digital camera probably compresses its pictures automatically into JPEG format ("Joint Photographic Experts Group"). Your scanner probably produces TIFs (Tagged Image File Format, acronym fans). Your image-editing software can deal with both of these type files, and many others. The main quest is to make the picture file size as small as possible without losing any quality. The main tool is trial and error. This whole process is known as optimization, although when you are dealing with poorly shot pictures it probably feels like "leastworstification." But that's the classic trade-off between quality and file size that the Internet creates. Deal with it!

Another file format is the GIF (Graphics Interchange Format), which deals mostly with images containing significant areas of flat color. So JPEG is likely to be your main weapon. First, establish the required size of the image (it's always measured in pixels, since you're dealing now with screen display). Then choose the amount of compression, moving the slider from low to high, hit *OK* when you're happy, and it's ready to take its place onscreen. When you see it again, it will have a ".jpg" tag (extension).

The Quality / File Size Trade-off

Whenever you save an image for the Web (when you optimize it) you need to get the file size down, so it doesn't take an age to load over a dial-up connection. This means losing some quality by "compressing" the amount of information in the file.

Saving Face

The original portrait *left* has a lot of subtle colors and a wide contrast range. The lit areas of the hat are completely white, and the pupils utterly black.

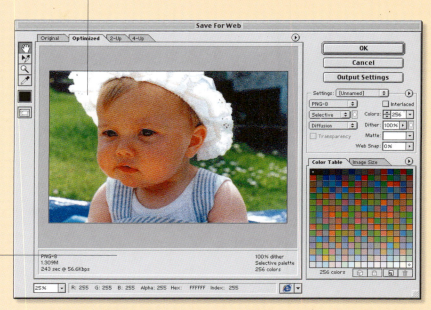

Trying too Hard

In the program window *above,* the original can be examined closely alongside a preview of the optimized version. Choosing "JPEG Low," though it makes a small and speedy file, is obviously wrong—the image begins to fill with ugly blocks that invade the light areas. You'll need to up the quality a bit—but watch that file size!

On the Edge

This solution (*JPEG Medium*, or 30 in the *Quality* dialog) is a good compromise between small file size and clarity. You don't have to know about file sizes and what they mean: a useful measure is to keep an eye on the timing note at the bottom of the optimization screen. This shows how long the picture would take to download via the (very) average modem. How long would *you* wait?

Now you have it all: a plan (remember those pencil sketches?); the picture selection all resized and optimized; some spare pictures in case the first selection needs amending; an idea about the words and maybe a background color scheme. Make sure all the pictures are in the same location on the computer to save needless navigation, and plunge in. You can try all this out without having any webspace of your own. Just set your browser to work "offline" and you can develop a miniature website like this completely independently of the Internet. You could equally well send the project to a friend by "attaching" the files to an email, or burn them onto CD. To actually "publish" your pages, however, you need webspace and a small piece of software which sends or "posts" them to the Internet. So, another set of initials: FTP (for File Transfer Protocol). This software takes your files directly to your webspace, and allows you to pull them down again whenever necessary for updating. There's normally a password system to prevent others interfering with your space. Some webpage programs and browsers have the FTP routine built in, but if not, there are freeware versions like Fetch (for the Mac) or CuteFTP which do the job just as well.

In any webpage program, there'll be a sample site. Look at the way it's put together, then try substituting your own pictures in their place.

A Web Address of Your Own
www.internic.org is just one of many Web authorities from which you can buy a URL (Internet address) of your own. Try it out, and follow the simple instructions you'll find there.

Greetings from the Country
Here's what you're aiming for: a simple, colorful home page that can take your friends and family (the ones you didn't invite) right there to your day in the park or the country. Simple links to each section will allow you to display your pictures topic by topic, and your visitors to navigate quickly.

The Robinson's Family Reunion
Woodsmill Park, Sunday September 7th

Mom & Dad   Our grandchildren   Our friends   The food!

The Moonfruit has Landed

If website-building software is too much of a giant leap, then take one small step by going to *www.moonfruit.com*. This is a simple, online service where you can build a website in an hour or two. It's easy: and you don't need programming skills or software.

How do I make a vignette?
See page 53
How do I make a link?
See page 64

PAGES, PAGES, PAGES GALORE

For your first Web project, keep it simple: just half a dozen pages or so. These will be enough to get a flavor of the event online—or onto a CD or an email attachment—and you can add or subtract as many pages as you like later. But for any of these projects, it's a good idea to test your webpage in more than one browser. Don't assume everyone has the same browser as you, as webpages have a nasty habit of appearing differently in different Web browsers, as we covered in the introduction, like Netscape (or Navigator), Internet Explorer (often known as "IE"), or rising star Opera (available from *www.opera.com*). Just follow the simple instructions in your website-building software about naming files, and you'll find that simple webpages like these, *left* and *right*, are easy to produce. Don't forget to link to the other pages on your home page.

A pet calendar

How old's your dog in dog years? When's her birthday? And when do your cat's nine lives begin all over again? (Don't forget that visit to the vet's tomorrow!) Paper-based calendars aren't just useful for keeping track of important dates and events, they make an ideal foil for your favorite prints. But when those calendars are digital and interactive, a whole world of possibilities opens up—and, being digital, you can edit them, reuse them next year with new dates, even print them onto posters, bed linen, or crockery (we'll show you how to do this later!). Many image-editing applications provide templates for creating calendars, and will merge these with your favorite shots. But did you realize that you've probably got a far more potent tool on your computer already? Excel, the spreadsheet part of Microsoft Office, can be used for making unique and individual calendar layouts, with all the functions of a spreadsheet. Take it easy: it's not all about tax returns.

Importing your images into Excel is as easy as clicking a button on the Picture toolbar. (If it's not visible you can display it by selecting the *Customize* option from the *Tools* menu. Check the *Picture* toolbar box and it will be added to the main toolbar at the top of the screen.) Use this to import your images, trim them (using the *Crop* command), and make fine adjustments. Once an image has been imported you can use its "handles" to alter the size to fit your calendar. Repositioning the image is just as easy. Click on the image and, holding down the mouse button, drag it to the required position. It's a dog's life.

GETTING RID OF UNWANTED DETAILS

If your pet photos are ready to use straight from the camera or scanner count yourself very lucky! Getting your pet to behave for the camera is difficult, and to pose—well, it might be impossible! So, many of your photos will need a little retouching prior to inclusion. Removing details—such as a steadying hand or foot (as here), or a distracting background—will make your photo more imposing. Go fetch!

The Cat's Whiskers

It's a good idea—even before you begin manipulating your images—to import them into Excel and place them approximately where you would like them to appear on the screen. You're not confined to a single photo per page, so experiment with different layouts. You can overlap, tile or combine your photos in the same manner as a collage. Just remember to leave space for the dates! Why not have a different cat each day?

Once you've selected your pet pictures (as it were), we can set about making them look even better. Remember that you—or anyone you give the calendar to—will be looking at the photo for a whole month, so there will be plenty of opportunities for criticism!

One of the best ways to emphasize the subject of your photo is to remove the surrounding background entirely—especially if your pet's not known for its tidiness. Image manipulation applications provide us with several ways of achieving this effect. One of the best is to use an image-extraction tool. Photoshop and Photoshop Elements offer the aptly named *Extract* command which makes the process very simple (*right*).

An alternative, found in most image applications, is to use the *Lasso* tool. You can use this to draw around the edge of the subject. Given that few of us have hands steady enough to draw an accurate, furry boundary, many applications offer a variation of the *Lasso* tool called the *Magnetic Lasso*. Rather than relying on freehand techniques, the *Magnetic Lasso* attaches itself to the edge of the subject automatically as you draw—roughly—around it. It is not entirely foolproof (it can be confused when there is more than one edge to follow) but with a little practice you can achieve very effective results indeed. And we'll bet there have been times when you wanted to lasso your pet.

If you have a pet with a *very* fluffy coat, you might find that neither method is able to select every hair, producing results that are more ragged than your dog. The solution here—if you plan to do a lot of this type of work—is to invest in a product such as Corel's Knockout. This is the tool professional digital image manipulators use for just this purpose.

IMAGE EXTRACTION

You can extract a subject from an image (lifting it from a distracting background) by using the *Extract* command. Here's how. Select *Extract* (from the *Filters* menu) to open the large dialogue box featuring the selected image. Draw around the edge of the subject using the *Extract* brush (the width of which can be varied to make the selection of "soft" edges much easier).

Once the selection is complete, you can test it (to ensure that there are no "holes" in the selection) and perform the extraction. You can then either use the extracted image as it is, or paste it onto your chosen background.

OTHER EFFECTS

Image extraction isn't the only way to emphasize the subject of your photo. Soft edges, blurring effects and even color changes can all help create a more effective image. In the case of the cat to the right we've applied a *Grain* filter to give a textured finish to the photo. For the photo of the dog (next to the cat) we've used the *Lasso* tool again, but then blurred the background. For a final flourish we've also applied a vignette (see page 52) to soften the edges.

Paws for thought? This combination of grainy and soft edge effects adds character to our canny cat.

Blurring the background (and the foot!) has focused attention on the subject, not your footwear.

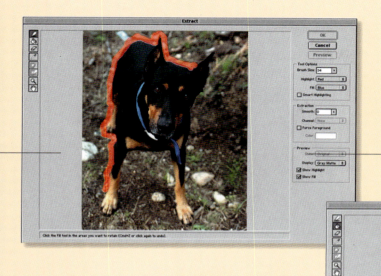

The *Extract* Dialogue

The dialogue box provides a range of controls to optimize the extraction process. You can choose the size of the brush and also the softness of the extraction. The latter control is ideal for subjects—like pets—that do not have a precisely defined edge. Unless it's a turtle... or a snake.

The Extracted Image

Once you've used the *Extract* command, you might be left with an image that still includes small parts of the background. Sometimes you can remove much of this by repeating the extraction, but reducing the softness level. Or you can use the *Clone* (*Rubber Stamp* in Photoshop versions), *Healing Brush*, or even a normal brush tool to paint over the ragged edges.

EXPOSURES WITH CLOSE-UP

When taking photos of your pets close up, there can be exposure problems when using some cameras. Flash exposure tends to be too great, resulting in a photo that is over-exposed. You can automatically correct much of this overexposure by using the *Fix* commands in most image editors, or simply altering the brightness and contrast sliders.

The *Elliptical Marquee*
Import the image into your image-editing application and draw the *Elliptical Marquee* across the head of the pet as we have here.

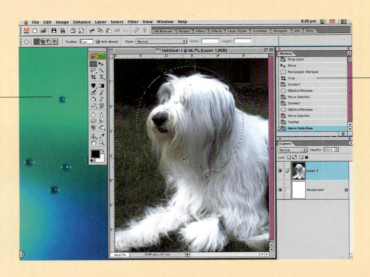

CREATING A VIGNETTE
We'll use this photo of an Old English sheepdog as the basis of a vignette portrait. This will produce a portrait of the dog's head that has a soft edge. When you place the image into your calendar, it will appear to blend seamlessly with the background. As we mentioned on page 50, this is also an ideal way of removing a distracting background.

OTHER SPREADSHEETS
Our example here has focused on the Excel spreadsheet, available as a standalone product and as part of Microsoft Office. We could equally have achieved similar results using other spreadsheet applications, such as Lotus 123 (it's owned by IBM, so it must work!) or the spreadsheet component of AppleWorks. If you have chosen to work using an integrated package (like AppleWorks) you'll also be able to use the drawing and painting components to create additional graphics for your production. These tools are particularly useful for embellishing the text and numerals in calendar dates. A range of presets enables colored and three-dimensional effects to be easily applied.

Excel is a great tool for calendar production, for three very good reasons. First, and most immediately obvious, it's laid out in a tabular, spreadsheet format: perfect for a calendar template. Second, it offers a wealth of data formats, including Excel database facilities (.dbs). And third, you can use some of its simple spreadsheet functionality to bring your calendar to life—even online on a website (you can save a spreadsheet as HTML). So, with a bit of imagination, and a very basic knowledge of math, you could set up each cell of the spreadsheet with different functions. You could have standard week and month tables or opt for something more avant-garde—such as a frame of days and dates around a central image. Using some of Excel's interactive calculating tools, you could create some even more abstract calendars. How about a calendar calibrated in dog years? Or a calendar page for each of your cat's nine lives? Just by clicking on a cell, which could represent a day of the week or a specific date, you could set up a simple calculation and "checksum": how old is your dog in

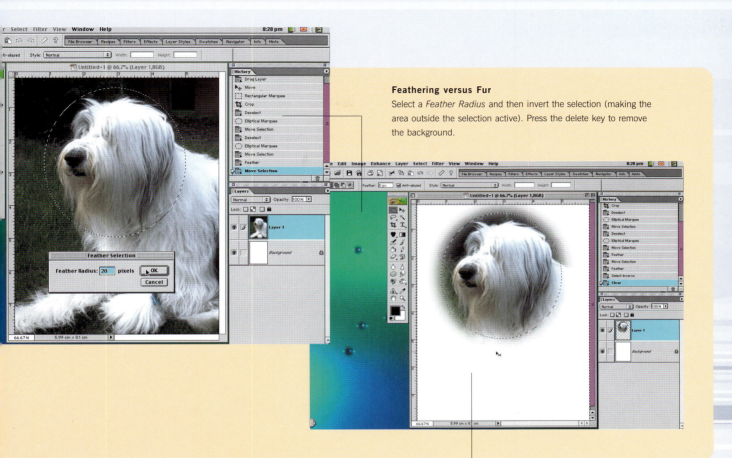

Feathering versus Fur

Select a *Feather Radius* and then invert the selection (making the area outside the selection active). Press the delete key to remove the background.

dog years today? How long since your cat's last visit to the vet? All in a dog day afternoon.

It's true that Excel is a professional tool and many of its features and concepts are designed for the advanced financial user. But don't let that put you off; the nature of Excel is such that if you don't need those high-powered tools, you don't see them! Stick with simple table construction and you'll have all the power you need. Then explore the text display features and examine how you can alter the look of your calendar with just a change of font or a little shading. Use the background color tool for those important vet dates (best done in pale gray to avoid worrying your pets!).

For colorful or dramatic text (to use as captions or to name the months) give Excel's WordArt a try. Simply select a WordArt style, type in your text and press *OK* to emblazon your page with text worthy of the most professional of signwriters.

Using your Vignette

Check the result. You need to ensure that the feathering has not affected the subject of the photo. When you are happy with the result you can use it in your calendar page... see page 55 for the result!

There's another group of applications that's ideal for constructing calendars: page layout software, or desktop publishing programs. These are the same applications that you'd use to produce your community, club, or society newsletters, and even national magazines and newspapers. The Big Daddy of these is QuarkXPress, the software used to create many of the publications you see every day. There's little that Quark—as it's generally referred to—can't do, but for our purposes it is probably too well specified. It's also phenomenally expensive, so avoid it unless you really need that kind of professional firepower. Other names to look for include InDesign from Adobe and PageMaker, originally by Aldus, but now also from Adobe. These are still professional products, but are comparatively simple to use for even a beginner. And they won't break the bank like QuarkXPress.

With page layout applications, you are far less limited in the way you can mix photos and text. You could, for example, have your calendar flowing around the vignette image we created on the previous spread. Or you could fade the image across the page and lay the calendar dates over the top. The only limit is your imagination, and you might want to track down some new typefaces. Try searching in Google for font websites. AppleWorks and Microsoft Works have ample layout capabilities, and you could do worse than use Microsoft Word.

Once you've created your calendar, don't be afraid to share it. It will look great on your wall, but give one to friends at the pet club or the local animal protection sanctuary and await the plaudits! Or publish it online, email them your Web address (URL) and wait for the visitors.

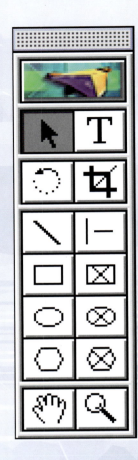

Seen them Before?

The tool boxes used by page layout applications such as PageMaker and QuarkXPress (*above*) feature many similar tools to those used in image-editing applications. Although getting to grips with every feature of these applications can take months, with a little practice you'll be able to exploit the key features required to create your calendar. All these programs—and their junior siblings—feature extensive online help and tutorial facilities, so getting your project correctly configured is pretty simple. You'll even find some examples to inspire you. So, get surfing!

TRANSFERRING DATA

Just as Microsoft Word's native data format has become the standard for document exchanges between computers and over the Web, so the Excel format (indicated by the file extension ".xls") has become the standard in spreadsheet exchanges. Even if you don't use Excel, there's a high probability that the application you do use will be able to understand a page from an Excel spreadsheet. Page layout applications tend to be more parochial. If you've used one of these, try saving it as a PDF (portable document file). Anyone with the freely available Acrobat reader from Adobe will be able to view (but not edit) your calendar pages. And they're often small enough to email to friends, and they're relatively easy to publish securely online.

A day to remember

Your finished calendar will not only be a work of art but a useful tool too. Now how about making one using pictures of your family… or favorite vacation destinations … or indeed anything you please?

m	t	w	t	f	s	s
1	2	3	4	5	6	7
8	9	10	11	12	13	14
15	16	17	18	19	20	21
22	23	24	25	26	27	28
29	30	31				october

Let's move house! and home page...

How do your friends get to your new house? And how do you tell the story of your day? Moving house scores highly on the stress scale, so photography will probably be the last thing on your mind in the flurry of activity on moving day. But, like all life-changing events, it's full of images that will make most families feel a lot happier about the event once the move is done. The necessary healing interval might be days, weeks, or even years, depending on the success of your particular migration, but you can be sure that a little planning in the premove period will bring great rewards. On these pages you'll find many tips that suggest alternatives and enhancements to the regular shots of comings and goings. And one more thing: make double sure that the box labeled "family photos" gets top priority safe handling. Otherwise you could be reconstructing your family history from other people's albums. And the key to this project, the key to your "moving home" page, is making something useful that you can email your friends and family members, or publish online. Just email them the Web address!

THE HOME PAGE OF YOUR DREAMS

Get the realtor to give you the flyer that first attracted you to your new home (the one with the captivating, sunlit picture and the carefully crafted words). If you bought your home through the Internet, download or screen-grab the page. If you're not feeling too happy about your buy, you could always compare the picture that attracted you, with one you took of the real thing.

The Right Direction

Whether your new location has pressed-steel or top-of-the-range carved stone, make sure you shoot the street sign.

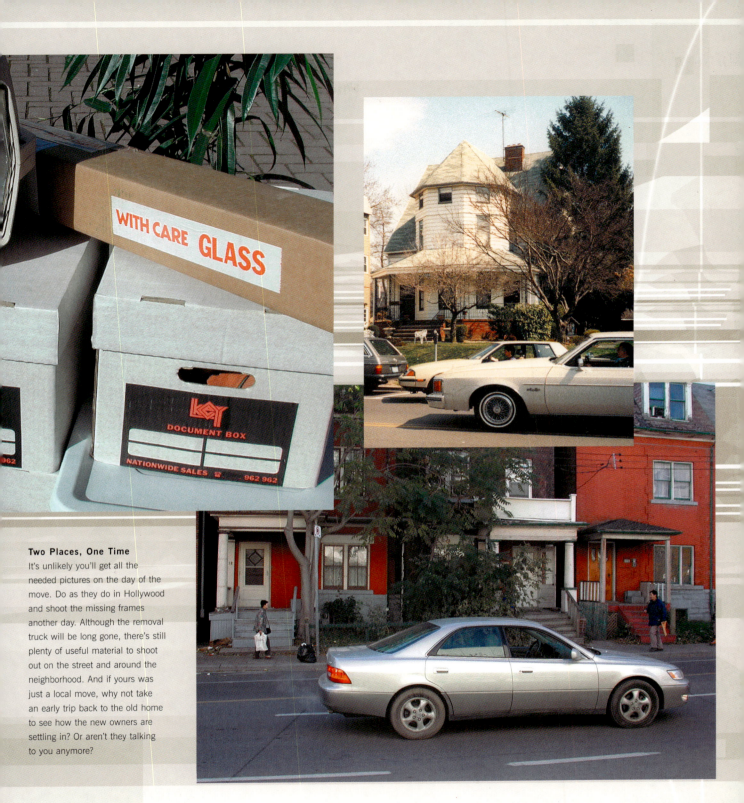

Two Places, One Time

It's unlikely you'll get all the needed pictures on the day of the move. Do as they do in Hollywood and shoot the missing frames another day. Although the removal truck will be long gone, there's still plenty of useful material to shoot out on the street and around the neighborhood. And if yours was just a local move, why not take an early trip back to the old home to see how the new owners are settling in? Or aren't they talking to you anymore?

If your move took you across the state line, or even to another country, you'll have a marvelous opportunity to create a real travelog (if you just moved one block, then some of the ideas on these pages will have to wait for the next big move). Remember that your audience may not be familiar with your new location—or even the old one for that matter. Look for maps, especially ones showing both locations. You'll find free maps at your new town hall, or the gas station. Standard printed cartography generally has an excess of detail—there are just too many contour lines and backwoods tracks. You could trace over such maps to simplify them, but most of that work has already been done for you by a new breed of Internet mapmakers. Try any of the route-planning Web sites, and you'll see examples of their work. These maps are kept deliberately simple since they are designed to be viewed, and printed out, at a wide range of magnifications. When you zoom right in to a locality, maybe a half-mile block, the map will generally change its character completely to show a much denser mass of information. All this material is there for your use—but check out the copyright box below just in case.

A QUICK GUIDE TO ONLINE MAP SERVICES

The mind of the mapmaker works in a different way from that of the map user. Where we want to know about miles-per-inch, the mapmaker prefers to deal in scale ratios. So it helps to know that 500,000:1 (five hundred thousand to one) is the same as around eight miles to the inch. The US Geological Survey state maps, for example, are produced at this scale. Let's say your move was 50 miles, and you're looking to fill most of an average webpage screen with a map that covers start and end locations (with some to spare at either end). So, 60 miles at eight miles to the inch gives you an image something over seven inches wide; easily accommodated in the average webpage. The largest scale normally available online is 5,000:1. At this scale your screen would show an area around half a mile across. Ideal for that move around the block!

BEWARE OF COPYRIGHT!

The license agreement for the map site on this page (*www.multimap.com*) runs to nearly 900 words. In brief, personal use of the maps is OK, but you must retain the maker's copyright byline and not represent them as your own work, or sell them. For other online map services for your part of the globe do a quick check on Google or elsewhere. There's too many to list here!

Internet Explorer

@ Map Centre

X=-13000000&Y=4000000&scale=20000000&width=700&height=400&gride=&gridn=&coordsys=mercator&db=US&overv   go

@ Microsoft MacTopia   @ Office for Macintosh   @ Internet Explorer

Click Here!

Free Maps&Links | Media Zone | Developers' Zone | Help

Directions   **Local Info**   **My Multimap**

NORWICH
UNION

RAMENTO

FRESNO

GLENDALE

ANAHEIM

NGELES

SAN

BEACH

PHOENIX

Homing In?

When you finally get your route
in your sights, there'll be a lot
of other items competing. Make
a screen grab of the map alone.

STOCKTON

Longfellow Drive

Green St

Fourth St

West Fifth St

SCHOOL

N

MALL

Lexington St

GOLF COURSE

It's time to put some meat on these bare bones. If you have some experience with an image-editing program, you are probably already thinking, "I can make a better map than the one I've just downloaded," and you probably can. One way to start is to print out the online version (just in black-and-white) and begin drawing over it with colored marker pens. Emphasize the areas that mean most to you in your old locality, and those that look attractive in the new one. Pretty soon you'll begin to see what's important to the story, and what can be left out. Take the opportunity to write all over this trial map as well—it's likely you'll trigger ideas for a whole new view of the move. Whether you redraw or simply reuse the maps you acquire, start thinking about the sequence of pages from the audience's point of view. You can zoom in or out, and shoot off down some interesting side streets and design alleys to vary the pace. If the move didn't go exactly to plan, include the disastrous diversions as well. Show, as here, a close-up view of the neighborhood superimposed on a small-scale general map of the whole region.

Now let's start making the online neighborhood your own! In your image-editing program, like Photoshop Elements and ImageReady, you could start "hot-spotting" your final map, and (perhaps in your website-building program instead) you could add links to the house images that link to a new webpage, or to interior shots of the rooms. Alternatively, hide a link under a map reference—such as Stockton in the map *opposite* —which takes you to a zoomed-in view, or to some local history text.

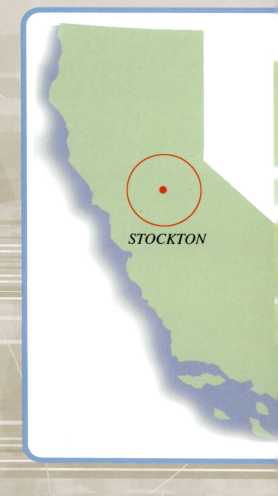

STOCKTON

DESIRABLE RESIDENCES

Look for landmarks. You may not pass Mount Rushmore on your trip, but there must be a notable sight somewhere in the region! As well as the vital shots of the homes at either end of the moving route, why not include some others along the way? You might, if you're very cunning, even use these impressive pictures to keep your audience guessing exactly which of these palatial dwellings is the final destination. You may be lucky and find your view unobstructed by vehicles and ugly utility poles; if not, you can extend your retouching skills by copying a bush or tree from another shot, and pasting it over the offending item (see page 81).

Butler Required
Can this be the one? A lofty lobby with chandelier would be delightful. Or maybe you're more of a Modernist.

Longfellow Drive

Green St

Fourth St

SCHOOL

West Fifth St

N

MALL

Lexington St

GOLF COURSE

A LITTLE LOCAL COLOR

The old conventions: water is blue; grass is green; built-up areas are vaguely brown; these serve well enough for regular maps. Why not make yours different? Why not make your house stand out in bright red? Your street in flaming yellow? Whatever you choose, keep it light and bright so that superimposed text can be easily read.

Using Layers

You can achieve the illusion of depth even with a simple image-editing program. Using a shadow under the coastline kicks it into relief. Try various treatments for the street map—this version has them cut out as white channels, but you could simply edge them with a darker color for greater contrast.

Decorator Required

Is this Xanadu? Maybe all that white paintwork will prove a problem. Didn't Madonna live here once?

Gardener Required

How to keep all those cars off the lawn? Disagreements might follow...

Lighthouse Keeper Required

Round rugs in the baronial tower? This could be journey's end. I see no ships!

Here are some more images that you can add to your map, whether it's destined for print, email, CD, or the Web. Welcome to the extraordinary world of clip-art. Again, you can use these to embellish a printed page or a simple emailed document (perhaps saved as a PDF or as a webpage), or you could use them to hide links to other, related webpages in an interactive project. Clip-art has a long history going back to the colorful fragments that children used to paste into scrapbooks a century ago. Then the clippings came free with soap or chocolate bars, now they come in their millions on CDs and on the Internet. The best CD collections prove to be very useful resources for those of us who can't draw; the worst make excellent coasters. There's no reason in any case for you to rely on the commercial product. You have the tools to make your own, far more interesting and personal collection. Flick through your old print albums looking for standout figures, pictures with signboards and posts, perhaps. All these, and many like them, can, with a little scanning, invention and trickery, be made into a useful treasury of instant humor to jazz up your project.

In this particular project, what's needed is direction, in every sense of the word. Pointers, arrows, and signposts for a start. Follow on with highway direction signs (and don't neglect the speed-restriction panels!). Once you've planted pictures on your map, they need to be tied to their locations with arrows or lines. Here we've drawn circles around the key spots, but the choice is yours. In a paint program it's easy to select a circular area, maybe soften the edges of the selection, and change the color to contrast with the background. You could even leave the small circular selections in color, and everything else in black and white.

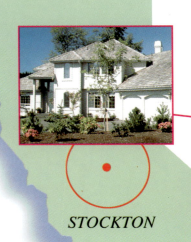

STOCKTON

USING CLIP-ART

Once you have one bit of art, you can easily multiply it. One clip-art door key (or why not scan your own?) can soon become a whole drawer of "hardware." Use them as decorative borders or backgrounds, along with squadrons of arrows. And don't forget the old favorites—the endlessly cheerful salesman and the impossibly elegant pointing hand.

Longfellow Drive

Green St

Fourth St

SCHOOL

West Fifth St

Lexington St

N

MALL

GOLF COURSE

PICTURE RESOLUTION

As you add more pictures to your basic layout, you'll begin to see the principle of resolution versus size. A project designed as a webpage demands an overall resolution of only 72 pixels per inch. Your eye in any case is deceived, by the brightness and saturated color of the screen, into thinking that everything is tack-sharp. By all means keep your prized, high-resolution camera shots safely stored away. Just make low-resolution copies and use them on screen. But you'll benefit from a higher resolution version if you're printing out your work as an invitation to that long-promised housewarming party, for example.

It's easy to develop your opening page into a linked series. Using Word, you can follow the *Web Page Wizard* (a humble *Assistant* in the most recent versions) or strike out on your own with *View* set to *Online Layout*. To get started, put a page together with some sample text, a couple of pictures (just hit *Insert>Picture>From File* to use some of your own) and maybe a colored background. Save this page as "Index," and be sure to save it in *Web Page* format, giving it the .htm suffix. Save it again as "Page 1." You can now change the elements on this second page while preserving the style of the first, and begin to create links between them.

For example, type "next page" at the foot of your "Index" page, highlight those words, and choose *Hyperlink* from the *Insert* menu. You'll see a dialog box that prompts you to locate "Index" in your folder. Select the correct file, then view the results with *Web Page Preview* in the toolbar. Repeat the operation for "Page 1," inserting something like "back to first page" as the text. Now you can rock back and forth between the two. If you have a dedicated website building program, the procedure is similar—see the software's instruction booklet for specific details. You can turn graphics into hyperlinks as well, or draw "buttons" in a paint program and add links and rollovers (see page 148) to those. You can use the *Table* function to organize your words, pictures, and graphics into manageable groups.

Now we're on the finishing straight. Experiment in your paint program to get an idea of what might work as a background. You might choose to stick with one dominant color theme, or to assemble a set of contrasting or matching colors. Select a typeface that looks elegant to you. If you're stuck for choice, go to *www.fonts.com*, *www.myfonts.com*, or try some of the wilder ones at *www.fontmonster.com*.

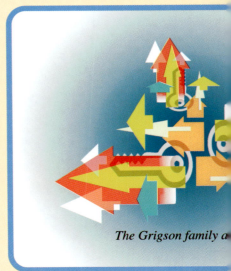

The Grigson family a

Arrows of Outrageous Fortune?
All the madness of moving house, symbolized by a swarm of arrows. Try setting up a link on the solitary one to take your visitor to the next page.

STOCKTON, HERE WE COME!
So much more arresting than the usual moving card, more personal, colorful, versatile, informative, and in every way more fun to do. Why doesn't everyone do this? Colorful graphics, maps that pop out of the screen, zooming changes of scale, buttons to push, all topped with an enticing invitation to your dreamhome. Great stuff, and easy to do.

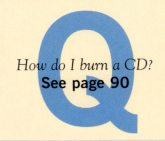

How do I burn a CD?
See page 90

BE KIND TO YOUR MODEM
Way back in this book we spoke about download speeds and file sizes. Now is when all those figures start to mean something! Your paint or Web design program will help you get this right. Let's review the basics. More colors or large images mean bigger files. Bigger files take longer to download and display. Longer download and display times make for grouchy audiences. The two weapons at your disposal are GIF and JPEG: the first is good at squashing down images with reasonably large areas of flat color, the second works best on photographs (or any tonal image). There are other formats too, such as TIFF (for print), or PNG (for Web graphics), but not all your potential visitors will be able to download a PNG.

... to Stockton, California...

The Big Picture
It looks like a short trip at this scale! But a graphic like this speaks volumes. Why not set up a link or rollover on the arrow, so the mileage flashes onscreen?

Home has Moved Away
The key is in the door, the drinks are on ice, and all's well in Longfellow Drive.

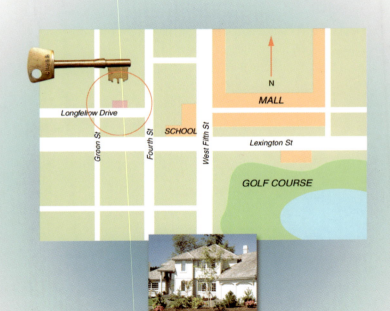

...1747 Longfellow Drive.
Housewarming Party July 8th!

Small office, Home office...

Now let's explore the possibilities of using your newly acquired skills in the context of a small or home-based business. Most big businesses are already wired up with sophisticated information technology systems and presentation software. But if you're thinking of setting up your own business at home, or already have one and want to use your technology to reach out to the wider community, your digital scrapbooking skills could be used to enhance presentations and win yourself new business. We've used the example of an independent accountant: just the type of business that can be run from home, but still have customers that demand professionalism and have a competitive market at their fingertips. Of course, the principles can be applied to whatever plans you have in mind! We've done two styles of presentation, using a variety of techniques.

You may already be familiar with PowerPoint software, possibly as a user, but much more likely as a viewer. Originally a tool for creating slide shows for projection, the results are now more usually seen as a sequence ❯ on a computer monitor, or repurposed as a Web presentation. It's the

ESTABLISHING A STYLE

Here we've imagined an accountancy company with an existing "corporate identity" (the brand and the logo that people come to associate with a company—just think of all the stores, diners, and sports companies in your neighborhood, and you've got the basic idea!). If you don't have a logo like your corporate peers, why not design one using your graphics program, or even your wordprocessor? Most brands' color and type set the style for all their publicity material, websites, and presentations. If you don't feel that such "serious looking" branding is right for you, try something a little more bright and cheerful.

MBP Accountants Online

PRESENTATION

Which Style is Right for You?

Assemble a few ideas and play around with them to see what works.
If you're stuck for illustrative material, you'll find there are numerous
searchable archives of images you can buy, or sometimes use for free.

dominant business presentation package, and offers beginners a helping hand with its crew of software *Assistants*, or *Wizards*. For example, there's the *AutoContent Wizard*, a template slide show that you can amend with your own words and images, so you don't have to set up new slides yourself. It's easy, and with a bit of perseverance you'll find it's also fun.

You can approach this type of project in exactly the same way as you plan your family album. Ask yourself: who is the intended audience? Is this a presentation to establish your credentials, or has it got a definite message? Sketch out the main points on paper and push them around until you see a structure emerging. Does the presentation need to be simple and colorful, or sophisticated and modern? We've done both.

If you choose to follow the basic slide show format, you can offer the viewer the opportunity to move freely forward or back, or skip screens, but the presentation will essentially be linear. But choose the interactive route, and the possibilities become much more interesting. You could offer two distinct pathways through the show: one giving an overview that offers a flavor of the business, the other your financial proposals, or business plan. Making links between these two gives viewers a richer experience, but it's up to you, the creator, to make sure they always know where they are within the presentation. The normal *Forward/Back/Home* commands are embedded in the program, but things will work better if you can provide a navigation system that appears on each screen.

Now it's time to begin finessing the introductory sequence. In our

MBP Accoun

Your way

YOUR BUSINESS safe in our hands

Flexible
Responsive
Experienced
Trustworthy

Presentation to Christopher Rye Music Inc

Images and Words
Balance words and images for maximum effect. Around 20 words suffice for this opener, combined with a striking and inviting graphic. A strong background color and uniform type treatment hold the whole screen together. Or do they?

Leave Nothing Out
Setting up the office shot is vital. The message is: we have technology in abundance and a relaxed working environment. Ergo, we can do good work for you—and be pleased to hear from you! But couldn't such images be used even better? See page 74!

WHERE'S THE ARTWORK?
Why not scan your existing business documents and use the image as a background for each slide, or turn any flat, scannable object you can find around your desk into a graphic you can reuse on every slide? Alternatively, why not do what we've done here and take some photos of your home office? For those all-important facts and figures, you can easily make graphs and charts in PowerPoint, or you can import them from Excel or another spreadsheet program. If you've got Microsoft's Office suite installed, all the software you need is right there on your machine already! But if none of this is for you and you want to put something together really quickly, you'll find that PowerPoint comes with a clip-art library (ValuePack), which contains over 7,000 items. This is a searchable resource: just tap in "success," for example, and your reward is 25 images of trophies, rosettes, and leaping figures. And it's not just images. There are movie clips and sound files as well. These won't be to everyone's taste, but like all digital material (as you are discovering) it's replaceable.

nts Online

financial security...

Show the Detail

It's not all technology. There are still people here with conventional diaries and a serious attitude. Our studious man at work here is actually "tele-working" from his local restaurant. Does he *never* stop work? Find out what more you can do with images like this on page 74!

first, bold colorful version, this "open door" graphic is a simple piece of
clip-art from PowerPoint's own collection: just draw a picture box, then
go to *Insert>Picture>Clip Art*. But you'll want to use your own photos,
graphics, and ideas, so go to *Insert>Picture>From File* (just make sure
you can remember where you saved your photos!).

Our graphic gives way to the draft company logotype in the second
slide. This transition is programmed in the *SlideShow* menu, which offers
41 different transition styles, as well as a *Random* setting to cycle through
them all. The simplest choices are a straight "cut" or a dissolve, but,
whichever you choose, resist the temptation to use more than two or
three styles in one presentation. It won't look professional!

The screen shown *right* is genuinely a "work in progress." The gray
logo appears in pride of place, but we've done a different version as well.
Design as many as you like and see which works best. Both were designed
in PowerPoint, but you could create one in your paint or image-editing
software, then import it into PowerPoint. The flexibility of programs like
this is there to be exploited, especially when it comes to choosing the
color and style of text and backgrounds. The embossed text appearance at

OUR WORK IN PROGRESS: CREATING THE LOGO

The "embossed" style makes a good starting point for producing a logo in
PowerPoint. Try imitating this example. The visual basis is simple: the smaller
type acts both as a subsidiary text and an underlining device for the larger.
Setting the main type color the same as the overall background, and selecting
"embossed" as the style, gives this impressive "low-relief" effect.

Accountants Online

Flexible
sponsive
perienced
stworthy

ristopher Rye Music Inc

the top of the screen is easily produced in PowerPoint's *Font* menu in a few seconds, where choices can also be made about typeface, size and alignment. The rest of the text is styled *Shadow* in the same menu. Above all, avoid typefaces with lots of fine strokes, as well as script styles. Always have the viewer's eyesight in mind when choosing type and color combinations. It's great to see vibrant colors onscreen, but the effect over several screens will frazzle sensitive eyeballs.

Next, for our first presentation, we've taken some pictures of a typical small office. Got the digital camera ready? Just download your shots and import them into PowerPoint as above. But straight away, you can see that the design doesn't work as well once the photos are in place. More about that later, in our second presentation style. But after playing around with logo and picture combinations, the screens begin to take on their final appearance, and the introduction of a chart projection recalls that this project has a serious intention. As long as you have the facts and figures, PowerPoint can generate graphs in a variety of styles, and you can also import them from Excel, if you wish.

This is a good time to consider that not every presentation has to be produced from the ground up using PowerPoint. Have a look at our second presentation on pages 74 and 75. You could use any wordprocessing or paint program to produce such a sequence of images. Import them into PowerPoint as full-screen images, and just use the presentation program as a "slide projector." And that's the key: you don't have to use PowerPoint just for serious business presentations. Why not use it as the basis for a slideshow of your new digital scrapbook projects?

Try Photoshop Elements, the cut-down version of Photoshop that we've mentioned before. The sequence of operations could go as follows: ❯ make a new document 512 pixels wide by 342 pixels high (this is

MBP Accountant
Your way in to finan

YOUR BUSINESS safe
in our hands

Flexible
Responsive
Experienced
Trustworthy

ACCO

Presentation to Christopher Rye Music Inc

GETTING DOWN TO BUSINESS

The progression evident on the previous page comes to fruition with the alternative logo integrated with an office picture. In PowerPoint, these different elements could be made to appear successively, fading in or flipping on like a light. PowerPoint lacks the ability to lock elements in position, and they're easily disturbed when you're working on the screens. It's better to use the strategy we've outlined in this project of using a layer-based image-editing program where such locking and alignment is routine, then import the results.

How do I add music and video to a slide show?
See page 94

LIES, DAMNED LIES . . . AND STATISTICS

Check out a few companies' graphs and charts. It's surprising how many of them don't show a full scale rising from zero on the upward axis. Although the cause might be space-saving, focusing on a narrow band of figures usually has the effect of accentuating small, upward fluctuations (in other words, it makes a small amount of growth look huge). If the statistics are not so good, a lot of companies create graphs that show them as small blips in a longer timeframe.

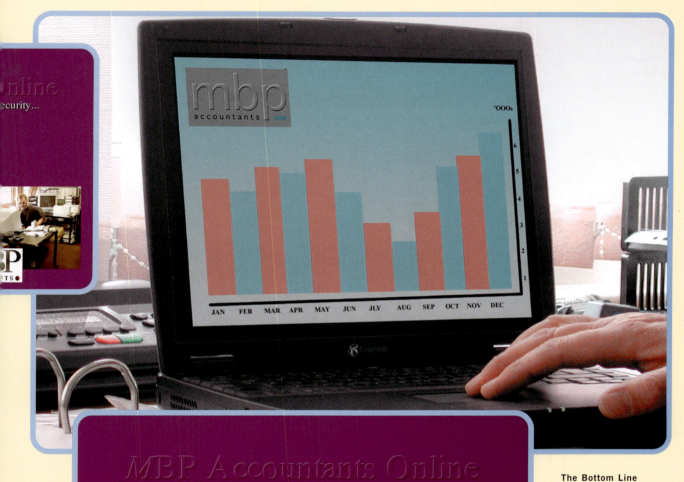

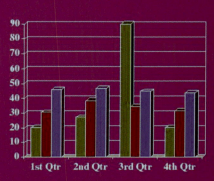

MBP Accountants Online

The Ryeworld plan for fiscal 2004… cash implications

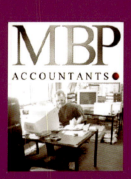

The Bottom Line

Our charts are generated, edited, and colored in Graph, part of PowerPoint. The import procedure is the same as for the pictures. Make sure that the color palette you use works well with the overall show.

CROPS, DETAILS, EFFECTS: OUR SECOND PRESENTATION

We think you'll agree this is much more like it: it's much simpler, much snappier, a touch more sophisticated—and far easier to do! Simply take a few pictures from interesting angles, or use your eagle eye to select the most interesting details to home in on and crop. We've used our man at work shot, then applied a *Posterize* effect to it. While you can do this in Photoshop Elements (Image>Adjust>*Posterize*), for example, we achieved this effect in a page layout program by changing the contrast (including the contrast between the colors). This creates an image we can use as a background. We've then added some other cropped pictures, and added some text on top. Simplicity itself!

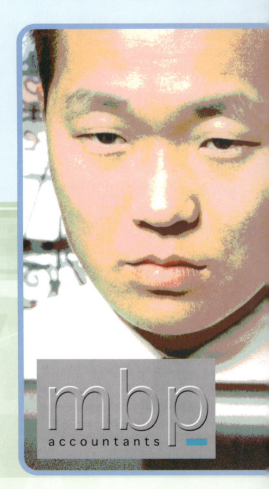

mbp
accountants

PowerPoint's "ideal slide format"); produce your artwork and type as required; save the result as a TIF file; import this into PowerPoint by selecting *Slides from File* in the *Insert* menu. Using Photoshop Elements' layers features may well make it easier to control positioning of re-used items, and it certainly opens up a much wider range of graphic effects than those found in PowerPoint. The same approach can obviously be used with any software capable of producing a TIF, JPEG, or EPS file. Try Painter, PaintShopPro, CorelDraw, Canvas, and so on.

Whichever style you decide on, it can be incorporated into a website, sent out by email, burned onto CD, printed out as paper prints, overhead transparencies, or even as slides! And if you want to use PowerPoint as the basis for a family album slideshow, or a digital presentation of your recent vacation, just follow the same tips.

PRESENTATION

RESIZING POWERPOINT
FOR REGULAR PRINT

Choose *Web Content* in the PowerPoint *Preferences*
dialog, and select *Picture*. Choose one of the two
large monitor options, 1800 x 1440 pixels, for
example. This is also a good setting for video
projection. When you save the show, also save a
copy as JPEG files. You'll get a folder full of
individual files which your conventional printer can
reinterpret as smaller, but higher-resolution images.

Wedding bells: online or video

If any event is guaranteed to get the photographer snapping and the video camera out of hibernation it is the wedding. The unique combination of setting, color, and emotion make for powerful images. But isn't it unfortunate that all too often such a momentous event is left to languish in a rarely viewed album, or on an anonymous videotape? So why not make your wedding photography—whether still, video, or both— something to remember? Over the next few pages we'll look at raising your photography above the rest, and how you can share the fruits of your efforts on videotape, CD, and the Web. The starting point of the project is, of course, the event itself. If you've been commissioned to photograph a wedding, make sure you go well equipped. A digital camera and video camera are essential, along with a good solid tripod and microphone. Never rely on the on-camera microphone for your important jobs.

A digital video camera is strongly recommended. Not only does it offer superb picture quality, it is the easiest to transfer to the computer. But don't worry if you've an analog model—we'll see later that there are ways of importing video from this too. Make sure you take plenty of spares—batteries, tapes, and memory cards. And though it doesn't deserve to be called a spare, a conventional SLR camera too.

Official Photographs
Official wedding photographs can be clichéd but, used with less formal shots, make an ideal basis for your production. This one was overzealous with that filter!

Informal Photos
Capture the formalities, of course, but also try and catch the bride and groom looking at their most relaxed, or crop to charming details like this.

WEDDING—OR WARNING—BELLS?

One of the great things about digital video is that it is easy to review. You can perform simple edits on your PC almost immediately. And if you have a well-specified laptop or notebook computer, you could even provide a preview screening during the reception. Take your notebook computer and you could even set up a webcam for those relatives unable to attend! But don't forget the smaller details: remember those spare batteries! Digital cameras and camcorders have a voracious appetite for power, rather like the best man. It is also a good idea to ensure that all batteries are fully charged, and to pack the relevant AC adaptors too. Perhaps use these when filming at the reception.

Group Photographs

Producing a set of group photographs is more or less obligatory for the official photographer. Photos of large groups, such as the one shown here, are an ideal way of ensuring that as many guests as possible are included in your production, including those who might not make their way to the reception. But getting everyone to keep their eyes open is another matter, lady in the white hat!

Spontaneous Shots

More so than official photos, spontaneous shots often capture the true atmosphere of the day. Don't worry if such photos are not perfect (they rarely are), you can always improve them digitally, as we'll explore in this project.

The Dance Floor

Like spontaneous photos, video of people dancing (or socializing generally) often provides some of the best memories of the reception. Video footage of family members dancing self-consciously is particularly prized, of course.

When photographing a wedding, it's a good idea to take a leaf from the book of the professional photographer. Work to a checklist. This is easy enough to compile and should include all the principal stages of the event. This way you'll always ensure that you are at the right place at the right time, and that you haven't missed anything crucial. And like the professional, don't skimp on the number of photos (or the amount of video footage) that you take. It is both easy (and desirable) to cut down the amount of material later, but it is impossible to recreate any parts that you missed.

If you're not allowed to video the service itself, use your video camera to record the sound of the service. Few will have objections to this. When you come to compile the movie, you can insert still images (that may have been taken before, during, or after the service) to provide the visuals. The audio track alone will be sufficient to trigger memories, while the stills will make up for the lack of "live" video. Prepare yourself for this by taking some "cutaway" shots—general views of the venue, floral displays, or even waiting guests—either as still or video footage that can be inserted into the "audio only" passages.

Cutaways are an excellent general-purpose resource. Not only can they be used to fill in sound-only passages, you can use them to link scenes, provide transitions, and even—when converted to still images— as titles on a webpage. You could also do the reverse, and create material —such as backgrounds and title shots—from still images. Often only a little manipulation is required (such as recropping images, or modifying the image, such as *opposite*, where we've picked out the bouquet.

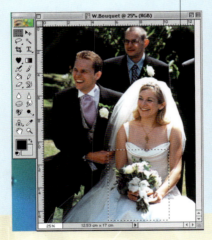

CATCHING THE BOUQUET

It is very useful to collect shots that can be used as titles on a website or video or to separate sections of your project into "chapters." When these have not been recorded during the event, it is easy to produce them from some of the other photographs you've collected. Here's a good case in point. The bride's bouquet, shown clearly in this group photo, makes an ideal detail to catch! The final image has a variety of uses: a "thank you card," perhaps; a page in your scrapbook; a webpage background.

Using the Magic Wand

Use different brush sizes with the *Background Eraser*: small is ideal for removing the fine detail around the bouquet itself and a larger one for the surrounding area. Rather than a background color, we want the space around the bouquet to be transparent. You can use the *Magic Wand* in Photoshop Elements to select the background color, then press the delete key to remove it, and leave only transparent space.

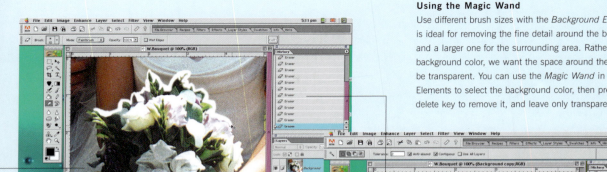

Removing the Background

Begin by importing the image into your image-editing application and zoom in on the bouquet. As you only require this part of the photo, crop the image reasonably tightly around the bouquet. You could use the *Extract* command, as on page 51, but this case lends itself to an alternative tool, the eraser. We can use this to erase parts of the scene and leave only a chosen background color in these areas.

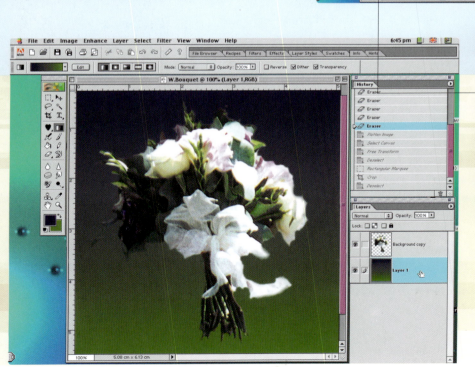

Adding a New Background

Now that the original background is transparent, you can add a new complementary background color. Add this as a background layer in your image-editing application. You can change the appearance of the scene merely by changing the background color. If you wish, you could even use a gradient or mix of colors.

When we look back at important events such as a wedding, we usually have a romanticized view. The weather was perfect (even if there was actually a howling gale), everyone was happy, and the setting was like a dream. But reviewing the photographs we are quickly reminded of the reality. Things were not entirely as we remembered! But with a little post-production work we can improve on that reality and put right many of the problems that are all too obvious in the photos.

The image enhancement techniques we use in such circumstances fall into two broad camps. In one there are the corrective measures. These amount to manipulating those photographs that have minor faults, such as being a little dull (underexposed), bright (overexposed), or otherwise suffering faults affecting the whole image. In most cases, these can easily be corrected, often using quick-fix commands such as *Auto Enhance* or *Auto Correct* (see pages 140 to 143).

In the other are those photos that are substantially perfect, but are in some minor way compromised. The photo *right* is a good example. The photographer has successfully "caught the moment" and recorded the intimate and memorable moment of the couple's kiss. Sadly, at this precise moment another guest has strolled by. Although the photo is still great, it would be much better if this person was removed from the scene so that the couple were truly the center of attention.

Fortunately we have the *Clone* (*Rubber Stamp* in Photoshop and Photoshop Elements) and *Healing Brush* tools, which enable the removal of the errant guest. Rather than removing superfluous detail by using tools like the background eraser, the *Clone* tool lets us cover up distractions by cloning—copying—other parts of the scene. It's a very powerful and versatile tool. You could also use it to clone material into the scene. For example, were one of the guests in a group photo to have blinked during the shot (and how often has this happened to you?) we could clone their open eyes from another shot into this image.

Some people find making overt changes such as these a little alarming. Wedding photographs are meant to be a record of the day's events and those events should be authentic. Most of us, though, want our wedding photographs to be as near perfect as possible. With your combined collections of official photographs, and those of guests, you have a wealth of material to choose from. And you could include a mix of "perfect" images (using image-editing techniques) and those that show a more authentic picture of the day's events.

Clone, Rubber Stamp, and Healing Tools
Clone tools are best described as painting tools. But, unlike other painting tools that use a solid color, they copy parts of the image, such as foliage here, and paint them to another.

Random Cloning
It is important that you select different "clone from" points when covering a large subject such as this. This creates a natural and random result, and avoids making the fix look too obvious. Pay particular attention to the boundary between cloned and original material.

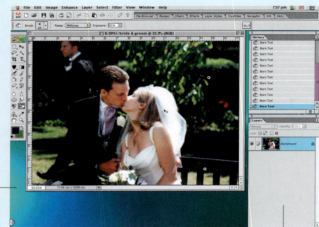

REMOVING A DISTRACTION!

Removing an unwanted element from a scene is an ideal use for clone tools. Here we'll use it to remove the guest who has innocently walked by at the precise moment that the photographer, concentrating on the bride and groom, took the photo. The photo itself is otherwise perfect and, even with the guest walking by, would make an excellent print. But notice how our corrected photo (bottom) is compositionally much more powerful.

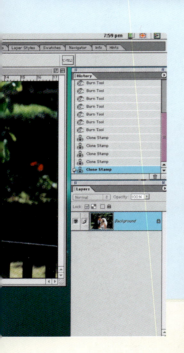

The Finished Portrait

There are no more signs of the passing guest, and the background looks authentic. A strong image is made even more potent with just a little remedial work. The professionals use these tricks too.

Those ad hoc photos taken at the reception, whether by you or other guests, often need a little more remedial action to make them look good. This is not necessarily because guests have poor photographic skills (mixtures of alcohol and emotion can compromise those skills!), but rather because the situations in which these photographs have been taken are not conducive to good results. Guests will, in general, be using compact cameras (whether digital or conventional), and will be aiming to make their own, informal record of the day.

Fortunately, most cameras today are capable of very good results, even when used in fully automatic mode. Hence many of the exposure problems that plagued earlier generations are gone. With small, but surprisingly powerful, flash units, photography in the dimly lit conditions of the reception are a cinch. But wait: flash brings its own problems. If you watch professional photographers in such situations you'll see that they tend to use a reflector, or flash units that are either mounted away from the camera, or angled upward to the ceiling. These lighting techniques give softer, less shadowed lighting that is more flattering to the subject. They also avoid two problems common to on-camera flash units: redeye and hotspots.

Redeye is a result of using a flash unit that is very close to the camera lens, hence the glowing eyes. Hotspots have a similar root cause. This time the light from the flash unit reflects strongly from the center of the scene (such as from a shiny wall in the background), producing lighting that is very uneven across the scene. Fortunately, both hotspots and redeye are easy to fix digitally.

The simplest way to remove this hotspot is to select the back wall and then replace it with a uniform color, based on the original. Use the *Lasso* to draw around the perimeter of the wall, with the selection boundary close to the subjects.

REDEYE

This photo shows where the power and direction of the flash has illuminated the blood vessels at the back of the subject's eyes. Many image-editing applications (such as Photoshop Elements, here) are equipped with redeye removal tools.

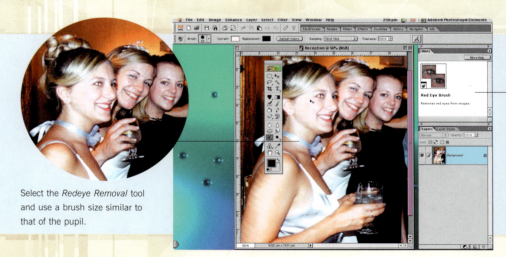

Select the *Redeye Removal* tool and use a brush size similar to that of the pupil.

COOLING DOWN THE HOTSPOTS

The direct flash light has here reflected off the wall behind the couple resulting in a bright and unsightly patch—a hotspot. Removing it will emphasize the subjects of the photo.

With only the wall selected, use the *Eyedropper* tool to sample the color of the wall away from the hotspot (over the bride's shoulder for example). Use this color to paint over the selection. In the finished print there is no sign of the hotspot yet the color remains authentic. A quick fix that won't be obvious.

By brushing over the pupil with the *Redeye Removal* tool the red glow is replaced with a more authentic dark gray. Notice that only the red has been replaced; the small white highlight —the twinkle—in the eye remains.

Once you've collected and, where appropriate, manipulated your images of the wedding you can set about building a webpage. As we've already explored, there are many proprietary applications designed for webpage—and website—building, but many image-editing applications also contain the tools for building simple sites. Virtually all of these enable the creation of pages using tools similar to those found in desktop publishing applications. You can lay your page out as you wish it to appear on screen. Once again, remember that any photographic images destined for Web use need to be saved in JPEG format, compressed to make them as small as possible without losing too much quality (it is useful to preview compressed JPEG images to ensure that they have not been overcompressed). Some applications enable you to view images as they will appear on the Web. This is a very useful feature.

Video-editing applications, including popular products such as Apple's iMovie and Roxio's VideoWave, often have the option of producing very compressed video footage that is designed to be posted on a website. While the quality of such material is not great, a short clip can be ideal for enlivening your site. Ten or 15 seconds—perhaps of confetti being thrown at the church door—is perfect.

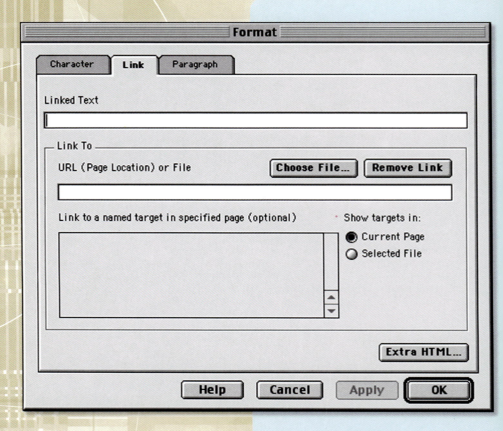

THE WEDDING WEBPAGE

Webpage-creation software provides the tools to create webpages that are as simple or as complex as you wish. It's a good idea, particularly if there are a lot of photographs, to provide a front page that offers fast and direct access to a particular section. And don't place too many photos on a single page. Images, even when optimized for the Web, will download slowly and you don't want visitors to give up in despair while waiting!

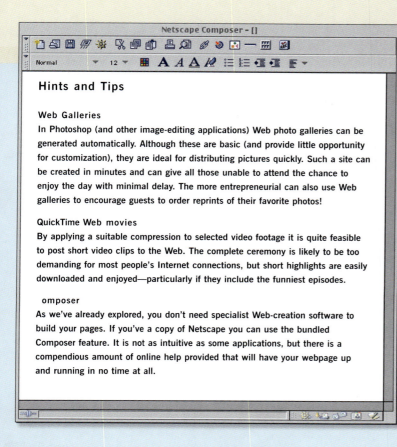

Hints and Tips

Web Galleries

In Photoshop (and other image-editing applications) Web photo galleries can be generated automatically. Although these are basic (and provide little opportunity for customization), they are ideal for distributing pictures quickly. Such a site can be created in minutes and can give all those unable to attend the chance to enjoy the day with minimal delay. The more entrepreneurial can also use Web galleries to encourage guests to order reprints of their favorite photos!

QuickTime Web movies

By applying a suitable compression to selected video footage it is quite feasible to post short video clips to the Web. The complete ceremony is likely to be too demanding for most people's Internet connections, but short highlights are easily downloaded and enjoyed—particularly if they include the funniest episodes.

Composer

As we've already explored, you don't need specialist Web-creation software to build your pages. If you've a copy of Netscape you can use the bundled Composer feature. It is not as intuitive as some applications, but there is a compendious amount of online help provided that will have your webpage up and running in no time at all.

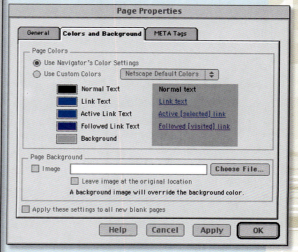

Links are the Thing

As we've touched on before, previously in relation to Word, links make the Web go around. Here in Netscape Composer above, the link creation process is as simple as a click or two. In this dialog, you can set up all your page's properties, such as background and link colors.

Hold the Front Page!

Here's an ideal front page for a website. A simple, uncluttered design makes it obvious what links have been provided. By clicking on the appropriate icon, visitors to the website can open separate photo galleries—including the bride and groom, bridesmaids, and friends and family. On this site an additional button starts the (appropriately compressed) video.

Editing the movie footage is probably simpler than editing the still images—so don't panic! Assuming you've used a digital video camera, you need only hook up the camera to the computer using a FireWire cable (called iLink by Sony) and start the software.

Applications such as the Mac-based iMovie (*shown here*) have made the creation of video movies simple. The software assumes control of the camera and will download chosen footage, dividing the scenes as the tape plays. VideoWave, from Roxio, is a similar product for Windows, while Adobe's Premiere is the big hitter for more serious users.

Once the clips have been captured, you can begin creating your own movie blockbuster. First drag clips to the timeline in the order you would like them to appear in the final production. At this stage you can delete unwanted footage and trim clips of superfluous material (don't worry—you are only deleting the copy on your computer, the original tape remains unaffected).

When you've got the sequence right you can begin adding transitions. Transitions define the way one scene blends into the next. Normally, one scene cuts straight to the next, but you can fade one into another, fade to black, or choose something more avant-garde!

You can also add titles—and even captions. For the titles you might want to overlay text onto a selected video clip (perhaps a scene-setting shot) or you can import the still images you made earlier as a background. Still images can also be imported and used alongside movie footage, either individually or as a slide show (see Project Five).

If you have used an analog video camera, you won't be able to directly import footage to the computer. You'll need an analog-to-digital converter (such as Dazzle's Hollywood Bridge or Formac's Studio) to convert the video signal first to a digital form. The digitized signal can then be imported—and split into clips—as above. See page 145 for more.

Step Aside, Mr Spielberg!

Simple "drag and drop" technology means digital video editing is now remarkably simple. Drag clips to the timeline in the preferred sequence and then add any effects or transitions required. Click on the *Play* button to watch your masterpiece unfold. iMovie, here, also permits two additional soundtracks to be mixed with the original video to provide background music, or perhaps narration. Once you've assembled your production you can copy the movie back to videotape, to CD or create a copy for the Web.

The beauty of using digital video is the quality. You can expect 500-line resolution, substantially more than offered by conventional VHS (around 240), and noticeably more than the so-called hi-band formats (S-VHS and Hi-8), which can only manage 400. And, unlike these formats, whose quality will drop further when edited, digital video loses virtually nothing in terms of quality even when intensively edited.

But there is a cost to this quality. When you download your video footage you'll notice your hard disk space is being consumed at a phenomenal rate. Using the DV video format (the most common digital video format), one minute's video will require 230 Megabytes of disk space. If you've an hour's worth of raw footage from your wedding, you'll need no less than 12 Gigabytes of free space to accommodate it! Even if you use Sony's microMV digital format you can expect an hour's video to swallow 6 Gigabytes of space.

Of course you are unlikely to use all the footage you download. There will be duplicated material, inappropriate footage (taken, for example, when you forgot to press the *Pause* button), and superfluous shots. These can—indeed *must*—be discarded. Your aim in producing your movie is to tell the story of the day's events. If you can do that in 15 minutes rather than 45, so much the better.

Although iMovie and VideoWave are effective applications, those with more serious aspirations may find the tools on offer a little limited. For these users there is a host of applications that provide a range of features that are similar to those used by broadcasting professionals. They command premium prices, but if you want to create a truly professional movie, these products (such as Adobe's Premiere and Apple's Final Cut Pro) are essential.

At the other end of the scale are the "generative" video editors, such as that offered with Sony's Vaio computer range, and by Roxio in its CineMatic application. These Windows applications can take your clips, selected music, and other preferences and edit the movie for you!

Adobe Premiere

Typical of the higher-level applications, programs such as Adobe Premiere allow multiple audio and video tracks to be mixed at will. The degree of control and the number of effects is substantially greater than on entry-level applications, which makes these packages ideal for the semi-professional user.

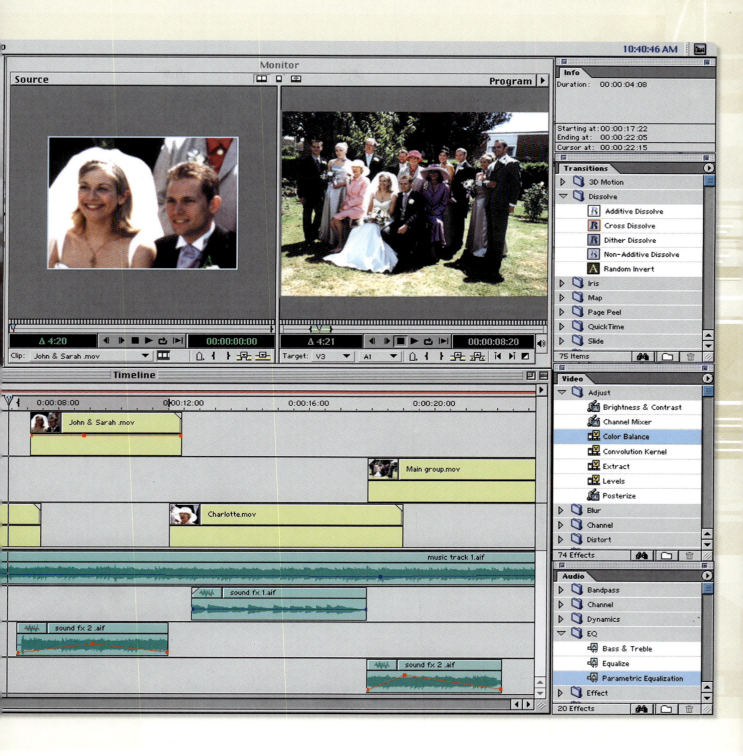

Using CDs as a distribution medium for your production is both viable and economic. A standard 650MB CD can hold a large collection of high-quality images and compressed movie footage. These can then be viewed on any computer and prints produced from selected images.

Using an application such as Roxio's Toast (Mac) or CD Burner (Windows) you need only drag and drop your folders of images onto the dialogue box to include them on the CD.

You can also use the same software to record VideoCDs and miniDVDs. Both these CD-based formats can be used for recording video onto a standard CD, which can then be replayed using a standard computer CD drive or a DVD player. Using the VideoCD format, you can store up to one hour's worth of VHS-quality video on a single CD. A miniDVD can contain only around 15 to 20 minutes' worth of video, but this will be at a quality similar to that of the source digital video material and DVD-video.

If you are fortunate to have access to a DVD-R drive, then you'll be able to create full-sized DVDs. With appropriate authoring software, such as iDVD (Mac) or DVDit! (Windows) you can create a DVD complete with chapters, animated menus, and featuring a dynamic mix of audio, video, and still images!

Your wedding production on DVD could, for example, contain the complete video in its original edited form (and quality) along with high-resolution photo albums and a host of additional material, such as guest lists and other ephemera.

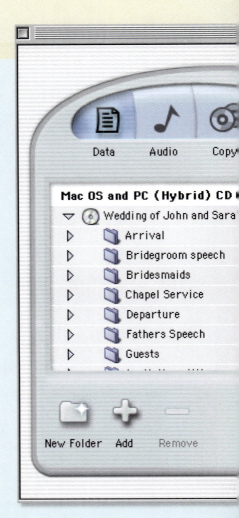

Creating your DVD
Applications like iDVD make DVD productions simple. By using simple menu selections and dragging and dropping screen elements, you can make a DVD video that is every bit as impressive as a commercially mastered product.

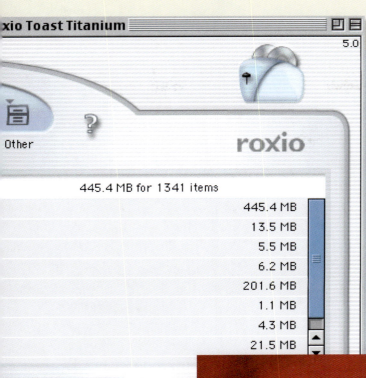

xio Toast Titanium

5.0

Other

?

roxio

445.4 MB for 1341 items

	445.4 MB
	13.5 MB
	5.5 MB
	6.2 MB
	201.6 MB
	1.1 MB
	4.3 MB
	21.5 MB

PX-W1210A - FireWire

THE WEDDING CD

Transferring your wedding video and photo collection to CD is simple and makes a very economic way of distributing the production. Talk to the bride and groom—they may commission you to produce one for each member of the family and selected guests as a "thank you" to them. Use a still for the cover, too!

Burning the CD

Writing files—whether photos, movies, webpages, or text—to a CD is simple, using applications such as Roxio's Toast (Mac). Drag selected files to the appropriate window, and press *Toast* or *Record*. After a few minutes your CD will have been recorded and verified (checked for errors).

Kidz @ play multimedia

After the rather formal and rigid structure of a wedding, a child's birthday party can come as something of a relief. There are no formal photos to take and no shooting script to follow to the letter. But that's not to say that you don't need to do a little forward planning. It's always a good idea to know the what, where and when of events to make sure you don't miss out on the fun. This is particularly important if you've been delegated as photographer, and are not the master of ceremonies!

You'll also be in the fortunate position that most children enjoy being photographed, and will be happy to pose for you—even if that means pulling faces. But you'll also need your skills to cajole those who are more camera shy: they (or at least their parents) will thank you for it afterwards.

It is the blowing out of the birthday candles that represents the high spot of the day, and this is where you could have problems, should you be covering the event with both still and video cameras. This could be the ideal time to appoint an assistant, as trying to operate two cameras simultaneously (and successfully) is impossible. Know your limitations!

Catch the Moment
Painted faces, a touching kiss. Photos that make children's birthday parties so special.

CAUGHT IN THE ACT
A children's entertainer makes for great photography, both still and video. Totally captivated by this balloon modeler, these children are at their most natural. Keeping your distance helps preserve the natural expressions and avoids the audience becoming self-conscious. Remember to vary your position when recording a video: no matter how compelling the performance the video will become tedious if it is all recorded as one continuous shot from one angle.

It's a Date

Add a simple title to the combined image and—most important—give the production a date! *Layer Effects* in Elements have been used here too, firstly to give the original image a glow (called an *Outer Glow* effect), and to give the text a *Bevel* appearance.

The Original Photo

The photo of the birthday boy blowing out the candle on the cake will make an ideal centerpiece for our cover, or for your scrapbook. We'll use the *Elliptical Marquee* in Photoshop Elements to select an oval vignette that we can paste onto a background of jelly beans!

MAKING A CD COVER

Memorable events call for memorable photos. You can use the photos you take on the day not only to create an album that can be stored on a CD, but to provide the cover for the CD too. Many image-editing applications include templates for producing CD covers (and others) that make getting the size right simple. Also watch for templates for creating labels for the CD itself. Why not get birthday boy or girl to draw the picture?

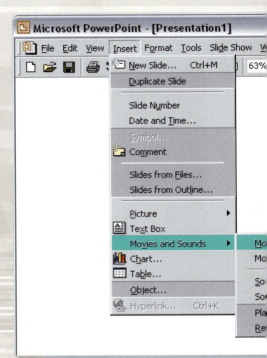

Whether you are using still or video cameras, don't forget that there is more to a birthday than just a party. You can photograph the child waking in the morning (usually very early!) and exploring for presents. And, at the end of the day, heading off to bed proud to be a year older, if not wiser. For moviemaking especially, these additional scenes help better tell the story of the day and really are appreciated in later years.

The idea of putting images onto CD is a good one. Despite the tendency to get scratched if mishandled or stored poorly, they have proved to be a very robust storage medium, and one that (despite the prices quoted for retail disks) is very economic. They also have the advantage of being compatible with just about every contemporary computer no matter what the flavor of operating system.

It is also (as we have mentioned earlier) a very simple matter to copy a large number of image files to a CD. This gives anyone who has a copy of the disk a chance to view, and even print the images. But a directory full of images is not the best of presentation styles. No, wouldn't it be better if we presented all the images as a slide show, and even set that slide show to music?

You'll find many image-editing software applications will generate slide shows for you. There are also applications like Power Show and, as we've seen already, PowerPoint, that are designed to do just that. Once you've created a slide show, you can create a copy that can be written to CD, or save it as HTML (under the *File* menu). In the case of CD, this copy includes a small player application that means anyone who received the CD can replay the production on the spot without other software.

When you create the slide show, you can determine how long each shot appears on screen (five seconds is usually ample), and introduce transitions. Like the transitions used on the wedding movies we discussed on page 90, transitions between the photos of our slide show make the change from one image to the next less abrupt. You can choose from a wide selection ranging from a gentle fade through to the wacky (and occasionally disturbing) mosaics and explosions. Like most way-out effects, extreme transitions should be rarely used.

Before sending your production to be burned as a CD or posted on the Web, you can add some music. A good soundtrack can really "make" your slide show, and there's no doubt it will make it more enjoyable to watch. And like the photos, you can add transitions to the soundtrack so the tempo of your chosen music matches that of the onscreen action.

Don't worry if your image editing application doesn't have a slide show feature. If you've Microsoft's Office, then you'll have a copy of PowerPoint. It is more than capable of producing competent (if unexceptional) slide shows of this kind, and can also incorporate music and even video clips.

Let's Put on the Show Right Here
Creating a slide show involves selecting a sequence of photos, placing transitions between the individual images, and adding some background music. The creation process often involves dragging and dropping images into a chosen sequence, then dropping a transitional effect between. After you've added your choice of music, your show is ready for burning to CD, or posting on the Web.

Gallery...
File...

Gallery...
File...
dio Track...
nd

MUSIC TO YOUR EARS

The choice of musical soundtrack for your slideshow can be a big problem. Your first choice will probably be to use something appropriate—such as your child's favorites, or even a collection of party songs. The problem with most commercially produced music is that it is copyrighted, and including it in your own production may contravene the copyright laws. If your show is designed for your family's consumption this should not pose a problem, but start distributing copies—even to close friends and family—and you could be in big trouble. It counts as a broadcast, or as piracy.

Don't worry. There are alternatives. You'll find that there are extensive collections of music available on CD that are variously described as "copyright free" or "royalty free," which will probably be ideal. There may still be some restrictions, so it is wise to check the reproduction license details prior to purchase. Otherwise, why not create your own background music—or better still, get your children to do it!

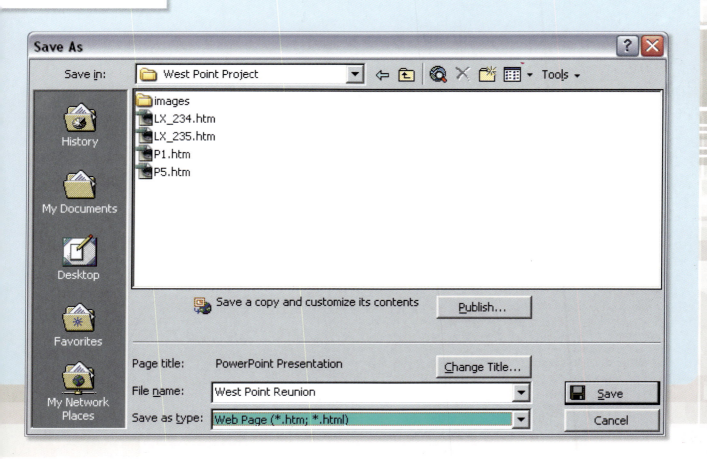

Bear necessities: record a collection

Whether our passion is model trains, cars, antiquarian books, or, as here, rare or antique toys, we all seem to have an insatiable desire to collect things. And, if we're successful, our collections run the risk of growing out of control! Digital technology gives you a whole new way of displaying your collection—and, if it is valuable in monetary terms, also of tracking your assets and maintaining effective records. So don't get lost in the woods!

The first step is an accurate photographic record. Isn't your collection photogenic? So wouldn't a photographic archive make an attractive addition to your collection? As we explored in the introduction to this book, the Internet gives you a unique and unparalleled opportunity to talk to other collectors, sharing your passions with like-minded individuals. With digital scrapbooking techniques, you can build a website, advertise your interest in acquiring new items, email pictures, or put together a CD—not to mention a traditional paper scrapbook.

This project will show you how to record the unique features of your pride and joy. An overall view makes a good opening page, but you'll need to record each item too, including its "pedigree," such as a maker's marque, hallmark, or—as in this collection—label, such as Steiff.

Bearing your All!

The simplest of photo records of a collection would involve nothing more than arranging them on the floor and taking a quick snap. But this hardly does justice to you, your passion, or your collection. Think of all the effort (and probably money) that has gone into building it and, by spending only a little more time, you can display your collection to better advantage. Show off the unique details of each that make them appealing, unique, or valuable. This in particular will provide the source material for an interactive webpage. See page 109 for our finished example!

THE IMPORTANCE OF PENCIL AND PAD

We all seem to hate spending time—or wasting time as we sometimes see it—planning. Whether our project is straightforward or complex, many of us like plunging straight in at the deep end. It's the same when we buy a new camera or computer, but fail to take time out to read the instructions. Only later do we discover that, had we done so, we would have found our new tool to be easier to use and far more powerful than we'd realized. So, spend just a little time noting down what you want to get from the record of your collection, and you'll be amazed at how much more effective your results will be. And as your collection grows, you won't find that you've painted yourself into a corner, by not having given your record any room for expansion.

Photographs of your collection need to serve two purposes. The first is an effective pictorial record. These will be photos that can stand alone in an album, or be used to illustrate a website. These make an attractive bonus for you, and could be your "shop window," if you wish, for other collectors or experts. The second is to provide an accompaniment to the written records that describe and define your collection—you've got the passion, so we're sure you have reams of written material on it! There is no reason why you should not take good-quality photos that serve both purposes.

For keeping an effective record of your collection, you need an effective framework. Microsoft Excel, and similar spreadsheets, are ideal. In project three we described some of the ways in which you can combine text information generated in Excel with photos. The process for creating an illustrated catalogue is similar, but this time you need to adopt a method of arranging and entering all your precious, hard-won data.

Arrange columns in the spreadsheet to list data relevant to the collection. For example, you might use basic column headings such as Item Name, Item Number (if you number your collection), Description, and Date Acquired. Other columns can be used to describe details that are appropriate to each item in the collection (such as details of distinguishing marks, notes about damage, color, or size).

For serious cataloguing tasks—and particularly where collections are extensive—there is a more powerful alternative to the spreadsheet: the database. Database software represents the next level up from the spreadsheet in the organizational process. Although not designed for many of the spreadsheets' calculation and numerical tasks, databases allow a much more flexible approach to data handling. You can produce custom layouts in much the same way as you might a handwritten record card, and like those cards you can decide how much space is devoted to a particular part of the record (known as a field). So, for instance, you need only give a little space to enter a date but can define a large text panel for entering detailed descriptions. Spreadsheets are much less effective in this respect. Databases really come into their own when you need to start searching. The rudimentary searching abilities of the spreadsheet are replaced with something altogether more powerful and comprehensive. Not only can we search for specific words but also we can search for groups of records that meet certain criteria. If, for our teddy bear collection, we wanted to find all those bears that are golden brown, were made between 1901 and 1919 in Germany, and are no more than 10 inches (25cm) tall, you need only issue the appropriate request!

Be a FileMaker Pro!

Not only do database catalogues look more professional than spreadsheets, the screen layout can be adapted to best fit the data required. Designing a database using the current crop of dedicated applications, such as FileMaker Pro (*pictured*), for Mac and Windows, is not as quick as customizing a spreadsheet, but it's just as simple. (Appleworks includes a cutdown version of the program). The power in the database comes from the comprehensive searching tools. Databases are used to catalogue the largest of collections, such as books in a library, photos in an image bank, and even office documents. Specialist image databases, such as Extensis' Portfolio, are ostensibly designed for cataloguing your collections of image files, but by using custom fields they can also be used to record your collection. You've the bonus with these of being able to keep track of your collection of photos too!

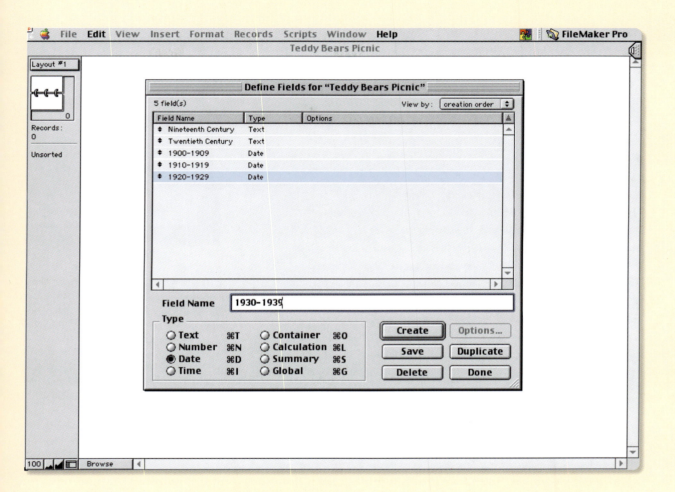

Spreading the Load?

Extensis' Portfolio is a visual database that you can adapt to use as a catalogue of your collection, including details of each item (*left*). Alternatively, although not visually the most appealing of catalogues, those created with Excel (*right*), or any other spreadsheet, at least enable the rapid entry of data. Combined with the possibility of adding images, they are an expedient solution to producing an inventory of your collection.

Photographing objects in your collection is really a form of portrait photography. And if you've ever attempted to take proper portraits, you'll be aware what a problem it can be to light the subjects well. But photos of your *objets d'art* do require slightly different treatment. Rather than trying to produce a portrait that captures a person's "essence," your aim here is to accurately record the subject neutrally. And the shadows that can give substance and form to portraits need to be banished, so that every possible detail of your subject is visible.

For a big collection, you'll save a lot of time by investing in a specialist lighting arrangement. Studio kits comprising two (or more) light sources along with stands, reflectors, and diffusers (which can be used in any number of possible configurations) are widely available, reasonably inexpensive, and work equally well for a table-top setup as for a studio. In our case we want to make particular use of the diffusers. These spread the light from our source (generally flashguns) over a wide area so that the subject is not at the mercy of hard shadows. Place one of these either side of the subject, and you'll have virtually "flat" lighting, which is ideal for these purposes.

What about backgrounds? If you've invested in specialist equipment you may also have been provided with one—or more—background screens. With names like "color fantasy," "forest leaves," or "desert skies," you may be tempted to enliven your photos by using them. Please don't! Your bears will be forever lost in the woods if you do. Although these are great for normal portraiture (and are the staple of many professional portrait studios), don't be tempted to apply such artistic flourishes. On a website in particular, they'll look cluttered and confusing. Stick to a plain, white background or, if you prefer, a soft, off-white. A plain background makes it much easier to view the subject, and will give you the flexibility to manipulate the shot digitally later.

The best way to achieve consistent lighting is to use a lighting cove. A white-sided enclosure (normally made of translucent Perspex), it is designed to provide shadowless, even lighting. Commercial photographers who need to photograph products for advertising or promotion normally use these. And although commercial models command the prices that professional users expect, only simple carpentry skills are needed to build one yourself. By fitting a translucent top (or even by having an open top) and painting the whole interior white, you can achieve similar, shadowless results for very little expenditure.

CHANGING THE BACKGROUND

You might not always want the same background for your photos. For example, you might want to color-code them on a website (using different colors for different decades or manufacturers). Here we've used the *Extract* tool again (see page 51). *Extract* is particularly useful for extracting our teddy bears, because it is adept at handling furry edges. Defining a sharp edge using a conventional selection tool is virtually impossible—you'll always retain some of the background between the hairs!

LEAVE ROOM FOR EXPANSION

Even if there are, ultimately, a finite number of objects to collect in your chosen field, it pays to keep your options open and allow for additional entries in the future. Whether you use a spreadsheet or database application, you'll be able to make additional entries easily (as new lines in the case of a spreadsheet, or new records for the database). With this in mind, it's important your catalogue will be able to accommodate future expansion—make sure that your planning has made allowance!

All Change!

Once you've extracted the image you can paste it onto any alternative. Note that there is no trace of the original light background—even in those "difficult" areas in the fur. You can experiment with different colors to find one that best suits the subject, but in general it is a good idea to go for softer and more muted colors.

Spending a little time in preparation shouldn't just apply to planning the project as a whole. Time spent preparing to take the photos themselves can pay real dividends too. An extensive collection is going to take time to photograph, and at times you will feel you're on something of a production line. And with large numbers of photos coming from your conveyor belt, you'll want to keep any postproduction image manipulation to a minimum.

But inevitably there will be a few little jobs that need attending to after you've finished photographing everything. They might include small changes to contrast and brightness levels (our "flat" lighting style is never 100% right for all subjects), and removing unwanted artifacts (like the fingers used for support in the illustrations opposite).

You could annotate your photos once you've pasted them into your spreadsheet or database, but you might also want to include captions on each image to give a unique reference or description. The filename of the photo is usually sufficient to describe the photo uniquely (matched with the corresponding record), but many people prefer the additional level of insurance that an onscreen identifier can provide. Adding text in your image-editing application, perhaps in combination with lines and arrows to highlight one or more features of the object, is particularly useful if you intend to share the photos with others. Adding text is easy, but you should ensure that the text size is sufficient to be read, yet not so large that it intrudes on the image. It should also be of a neutral color that makes it easily read. "Sans serif" fonts (those like Arial and Verdana that have "clean" edges) are the easiest to read onscreen and are preferable to "serif" fonts (like Times and New Century Schoolbook), whose tails and flourishes often make them harder to read on a computer monitor.

SHADOWS ARE YOUR ENEMIES!

It's crucial to avoid shadows when taking photos of your collection, and the same applies if you're going to use these shots in a simple animation—even more on this shortly! But for a simple "movie" of one of your collection, flat lighting is no longer sufficient; you'll need to move your diffused light sources further to the sides and introduce another to the front, in line with the camera. Viewed in isolation, the results you'll get from this form of lighting look a little absurd; it is shadows, after all, that help create the illusion of three dimensionality in the subject. But don't worry though. When compiled into a sequence the shots will look fine! See page 107.

CHECK BEFORE TAKING THE PICTURES

How many times have you taken a photo only to find when you examine the results that you've committed some howling gaff? That tree apparently growing out of someone's head, or that missing limb, are just two examples of defects that could so easily have been recognized when composing or arranging the shot. When you're photographing your collection it pays to be equally vigilant. Don't just check in the viewfinder once; check again. And if you are using a digital camera, review your shots periodically so that you can correct any deficient images quickly. You will be able to fix many problems digitally later, but why bother when you can get things right in the first place!

REMOVING UNWANTED DETAILS

Sometimes you've no alternative. To display your objects to best effect you might need to use an improvised stand, or even, as here, a steadying hand. Removing the evidence is simple—if you've taken our advice and used a plain white background! Here we've used a *Clone* (or *Rubber Stamp*) tool in our image editor to copy color from the background over the hand. Getting a good clean edge is easier if you use a selection tool to define the clone area.

There was no alternative to a steadying hand here, but...

...a little work with the *Clone* tool gives teddy all the support he needs!

PHOTOGRAPHIC HINTS AND TIPS (FOR MORE, SEE PAGES 134-137!)

THE LONGER VIEW

What is the best lens—or the best focal length to use when photographing your collection? Many cameras feature a modest, wide-angle lens as standard, which is ideal for capturing wide, sweeping landscapes or group photos in a confined space. Unfortunately, these are not ideal for photographing objects in your collection. Wide-angle lenses tend to exaggerate perspective. Faces, in particular, look unusually round when taken in close up, and although it might not be immediately obvious, the same problem will affect the photos in your collection. It's better to use a basic telephoto lens. If you are using a 35mm camera, look for focal lengths between 80mm and 125mm. On digital cameras (or compact cameras) with zoom lenses you'll need to set an intermediate focal length around two thirds of the way from the wide-angle setting (the precise focal length is not critical).

GET IN CLOSE

Most digital cameras feature a useful *Macro* setting that lets you get in really close to your subject. Switching to macro lets you fill the frame with a tiny detail, and if your collection already features small items (perhaps jewelry, or even stamps) you could find that the *Macro* setting is more or less essential for filling the frame with each object.

A SENSE OF SCALE

The downside of photographing each object in isolation is that you lose the sense of scale, and it is impossible to tell how large any item is. Consider placing something in the scene that restores the sense of scale. It could be a clearly visible rule or, for smaller subjects, a coin. If you collect vintage cars, steam engines, or boats, of course, you'll need thousands of coins to start with!

The trouble with the photos we take for record purposes is that they are —to be frank—a little dull! Of course this, as we explained, is borne of necessity. But collections are there to be enjoyed, so why not make the best of them? Okay, so we've already shown how a photograph of our collected teddies has almost no photographic merit, but you can create some very effective alternatives!

One way is to create "virtual shelves." Once you've taken all your "catalog" photographs, you can line up all those standard, face-on views and blend them together seamlessly into a wide, panorama-style shot without any editing. And hope no one sees the join! The consistent lighting and plain background should make this simple to construct. But an even easier way to compile selected images into a panorama is to use panoramic software—which would be particularly effective if you collect cars, for example, and line them up outside. But let's stick with our teddy bears! There are several economically priced packages designed for merging individual images into a seamless panorama (such as Roxio's PhotoVista), while many image editing programs (including Roxio's PhotoSuite, and Adobe's Photoshop Elements) have the feature built in.

Panoramic software can automatically identify common features in adjacent photos and blend them together. As our bear photos have no common elements (save for the white space), the feature will be unable to interpret the photos we've provided, but it may work for your collection. In our case, we had to manually adjust the subjects' relative positions. But with little effort, here's the result, *below*!

The Usual Suspects
Below Despite comprising eight individual photos, the resulting "panorama" suggests that all eight were in the same line-up. So which one do you think hit Goldilocks?

STITCHING IN TIME

Panoramic software may be easy to use, but there are some complex calculations going on behind the scenes. For best results, you'll need to identify the focal length of the lens used to take the photos (perspective corrections differ with focal length) and provide a significant (around 30%) overlap between adjacent scenes. This gives the software something to lock onto when linking images. Joining the images—called stitching—is an automatic process, but most programs allow some manual intervention. This can be critical in cases where the software is unable to identify common points, or is confused by repeating patterns or similar features. If your panorama is wide enough, you can even produce a 360-degree view. When viewed onscreen you can circle continuously through your collection—and so can your website visitors if you post it online!

Whether strictly for recording purposes or more artistic interpretations, our object photographs only provide single viewpoints. You could include additional shots that show what lies around the back, but wouldn't it be great if you could display an object from any angle? Well, you can!

You can do this using Virtual Reality technology. This isn't the virtual reality that involves wearing special gloves and headsets, but thankfully (unless you like dressing up) a practical desktop variation.

This technology, made popular by Apple through its QuickTime VR software, allows the viewing of two types of virtual reality environments ("movies")—panoramas and objects. Both comprise still images. Panoramas are similar to the one we created on the previous page, except that when viewed through an appropriate player, the viewer can choose to move around the scene and even zoom in or out on certain elements. It puts you in the picture, at the center of the action!

Object virtual reality movies place an object at the center and, as if it were on a turntable, let you rotate it to view from all angles. When you view a virtual reality object, the mouse pointer becomes a grab hand. Click with your mouse button and you can use this to drag the object around (nominally round a vertical axis, although triple axis all-direction rotations are possible too).

Creating an object movie involves photographing the object and then moving it around by a few degrees and taking another. You repeat until the full 360 degrees have been covered. The more photographs you take the smoother the movements will be when the movie is played. At ten-degree increments the movie will be very jerky, while using two degrees will give a very smooth result (albeit with a large file size!).

Producing successful virtual reality is a complex process, but there are easier (and often equally effective) alternatives that you can attempt, such as the movie animation we describe, *right*.

Round and Round
For a genuine VR movie, you'll need to photograph each object from every angle. Placing it on a turntable can help here. Flat, shadowless lighting is essential to prevent strange artifacts (known as banding transients) spoiling the quality of the movie.

MOVIES IN THE ROUND

Creating "real" virtual reality movies is not that simple, and it can also be a laborious process. You can, however, achieve a very similar result by building an animation sequence based on a sequence of photos. By using each consecutive photo as a frame of the animation and getting the resulting movie to loop continuously, you'll get an impressive effect. You could use an animation generator for this (such as Animation Shop, supplied with PaintShop Pro) or, for best results, a movie-editing application. Import each still image as a new video clip, and set each to display for a short time (0.1 or 0.2 seconds).

When you've finished recording your collection, you might be surprised at how valuable a resource you've created. If your collection is of obscure items of minor monetary value, you'll discover there are many other collectors out there. Be a collector of things of more bankable value, and you may find there are many more people interested in sharing your data.

The easiest way to share information is to create a webpage. And as you've already created the photos to illustrate it and gathered the technical details, it will just be a matter of putting these together on the page.

It's important that the webpage is constructed in a way that makes it easy (and obvious) for any visitor to navigate. Many a potentially useful site has been compromised by poor navigational tools, which make it impossible for visitors to get from one point to another in a logical manner. Website visitors have expectations based on the sites that they've visited, and they'll have scant patience for anything that is not equally as slick!

Don't forget your website could contain not only the images you've created, but any research documentation you've found and links to other relevant websites. And if you've been bold enough to create a virtual reality movie (or animation) why not include those too? Or your database? You could even consider including some video clips if the items in your collection are in any way "animated." Even items such as "transforming" toys will benefit from the movie treatment, showing how they operate or change. It's easy: just set your video camera on a tripod and record the action!

DAY OF RECKONING

Your records could well have an unexpected use should something unfortunate happen to your collection. If you're unlucky enough to be robbed, suffer a fire, or some other material loss, then proving your loss to insurers and their adjusters could be a huge problem. How do you demonstrate the scope and nature of your collection, when there's no hard evidence of its existence? Your database and the photos in it could come to your assistance. Although they won't prove beyond doubt the details of your collection, they'll go a long way to help you make good. In fact, this is a good reason why you should make an inventory of your whole house. Obviously, it's not feasible to list every possession, but you can record much of the content in comparatively few photos.

Details ○

1920-29   *1930-39*   *1940-48*   *1960-66*

Growing a family tree

Whether you're looking into your roots, seeking out an illustrious ancestor, or just plain curious, genealogy has never been more popular. And of all its aspects, the creation of a family tree has never been so easy. The Internet has given us the opportunity to email friends and family—or even see them, via a webcam—as often as we wish. And this same technology has made it easy to trace family members, both past and present. So great is the range of information now available to us that you can go well beyond the traditional family tree and construct elaborate histories, complete with photos, videos, and documented details of work and home life. And with your newly honed digital scrapbook skills, you can bring your ancestors back to life! Although the Web has provided a great many resources for the family history researcher, by no means all your material will arrive in this way. Most will come from current family members. Just think of the number of photo albums, many dating back decades, that are in the family. These are the ideal basis for your next project!

Check those Shoeboxes

Those forgotten or archived boxes of old documents—collected in old shoeboxes, perhaps, or gathered from a house clearance—are a great source of information. Birth certificates and letters are an obvious source of important information, but other saved documents can give intriguing insights into the way your forebears lived. Something as humble as a bank statement could be a goldmine (literally, we hope!). You'll see how much your distant relatives were paid and how they used their money—even who they traded with. And wartime documents might give an insight into their lives through their darkest days. Receipts can provide useful provenance on family heirlooms—some of which may be in your possession today.

DON'T FORGET OLD HOME MOVIES!

Old collections of home movies are an ideal resource for discovering more about your—and your ancestors'—pasts. They will be full of family gatherings, social events, and travel footage that can give you valuable insights into your roots. And think of the resource you can leave your descendants! Why not hold a movie night and invite family members along? You can use the event to help identify your own movie's stars and give further substance to your family tree project. It's also a good idea to transfer old movies to video (digital video is best). Give posterity a chance!

Picture Collections

Picture collections could be the backbone of your family tree project. Not only do they provide a glimpse of long-departed relatives, they're useful documents that show the way your predecessors lived—and dressed. Get the hair!

For many researching their family history, the excitement comes from the detective work. It will involve not only a search through family archives (which, in general, tend to extend to only a few generations), but local governmental agencies and church records (which tend to hold much of the historical data in many Christian traditions).

Gathering information from the Internet can be a problem—it isn't yet a cure-all for all information ills. If you perform a simple surname search using one of the more comprehensive search engines (such as Google, AltaVista, or Lycos), you're likely to get thousands of "hits" (even for less common surnames), most of which will be irrelevant.

So, as we covered in the introduction to this book, you'll need to be more focused. If you know your family has some roots in a particular location, search using both your surname and that location as keywords. You can also use one of the excellent genealogy portal sites, which link to sometimes hundreds of other resources. These links and access points to further sites enable you to conduct a very precise and detailed investigation. *Cyndi's List* (*far right*) is a good example, but check out About.com too.

It also pays to be proactive. Set up your own website and invite others—perhaps distant relations investigating their own ancestry—to contribute. By including in the keyword section of your site certain keywords (including surname, ancestors' names, and home towns) you can attract visitors who are using these very same keywords as part of their own searches. The aim is to inform others of your presence and get as much pertinent information as possible. Even a couple of paragraphs of text and some photos should be ample.

IF YOU DON'T ASK, YOU DON'T GET

Not all your information will be presented to you on the proverbial plate. You'll need to do some asking, and—in a few cases—begging! When the begging needs to be done of relatives, assure them that the valued documents or photos you're asking to borrow will be copied and the originals returned to them undamaged. Official records are often freely available—if you know where and who to ask. Depending on where you live, copies from the records kept by local, state, and federal government agencies can be obtained relatively easily. Those from churches and other nonstatutory organizations may involve a little cajoling. Perhaps a contribution to the upkeep of the church might help!

Colls of

Henry Colls of North Elmham
B
D. 1641   M. 1628 to Elizabeth

William Colls of North Elmham
B 1632   Husbandman.
M.1660 to Joanne [neé Boyder
D 1673

William Colls of North Elmh
B 1664   Water-mill owner at
                and later at Aldb
M - 1691 — Mary neé Boyder
D -1740   at Aldborough

Robert Colls of Itteringham
          Water-mill owner
B 1708 at Burgh   Left hi
M - Hannah — B 1712 D 1800
D - 1777

John Colls of Horstead marri
B. 1744   Water-mill owner
M. 1767   at Horstead
D 1806   Grave stone on floor
                of Horstead church
                just inside door, on
                right.

John Colls of Gt Yarmouth Ma
B 1771   Merchant.
M.1805 to Ann neé Weeds
          Daughter of Capt. James

Windows on your World

Genealogical portal sites are a great way of beginning your investigations, and can alert you to new resources.

Yolk, England.

andman

ary Colls
B 1630
M. 1705
To William Banbury

Prudence
Colls

Elizabeth
Colls

FROM LITTLE ACORNS... FAMILY TREES WILL GROW

You may be fortunate enough to discover that your whole family tree has already been compiled by a zealous relative, but if not there is a good chance that some parts of it have indeed been documented. Such works could be residing in an official resource—such as local governmental offices or record offices—just waiting for you to uncover them. Others may have already found their way onto the Web. Of course, how easy it is to find the information will depend on your surname— if your surname is relatively common, you'll be facing much more of an uphill struggle to sift your relatives' details from those of thousands of unrelated strangers. It's very likely that your investigations will ultimately produce a mix of historic documents and Web-delivered material.

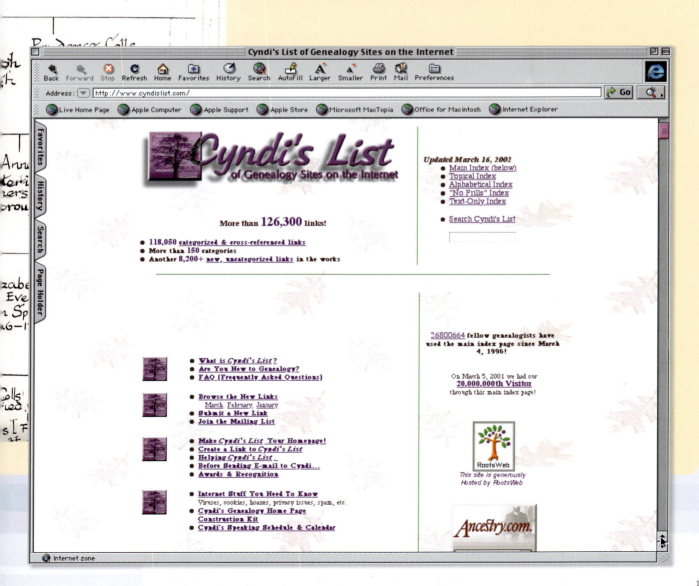

As your investigations continue, you're likely to come up against some obstacles. Some of these will be difficult to overcome. There might, for example, be an abrupt break in the records, or the records might themselves be missing or have been destroyed. Others will be a simple challenge, such as the discovery that your ancestors or relatives had emigrated to or from other countries. Clearly, it's not feasible to visit each of these countries and continue your enquiries directly, so you'll have an ideal opportunity to test your Web-investigative skills!

Some of the larger Web portals can give useful pointers to websites to explore in other countries. A useful feature of many portal sites is their database collections. These list databases of official records—ranging from national census surveys, through to local parish and probate records that are available online and can be browsed by the researcher. Ancestry.com, for example, lists (or provides access to lists of) more than 1.5 billion names of people in the English-speaking world and certain other territories. You can search through census records, military records, the Land Registry and Probate Office (for those with British ancestry), Civil War records, and more—much, much more.

Gathering information from so many sources is almost guaranteed to produce results. But if you are particularly successful, and discover a great number of relatives and ancestors, how far back should you go and how many strands of your family should you include? In many respects that's a very personal question. People have their own reasons for delving into their pasts, but as a rule of thumb most people tend to construct family trees that are deeper than they are broad. So you will find more generations—the "depth" of the tree—listed than parallel strands, which are those parts of the tree populated by "removed" cousins and the like, who comprise the "breadth" of the tree. People, it seems, are keener on seeing where and who they came from than discovering where distant cousins are now. Of course, there are exceptions. If you are convinced you are a distant relative of royalty, or share the genes of those in political power, broad trees will be essential.

Under one Roof

Websites like Ancestry.com act as both portal and search engine. It makes good sense to bookmark these sites as new material and extended resources appear all the time. Make a repeat visit and you may find that crucial database you have been awaiting has arrived.

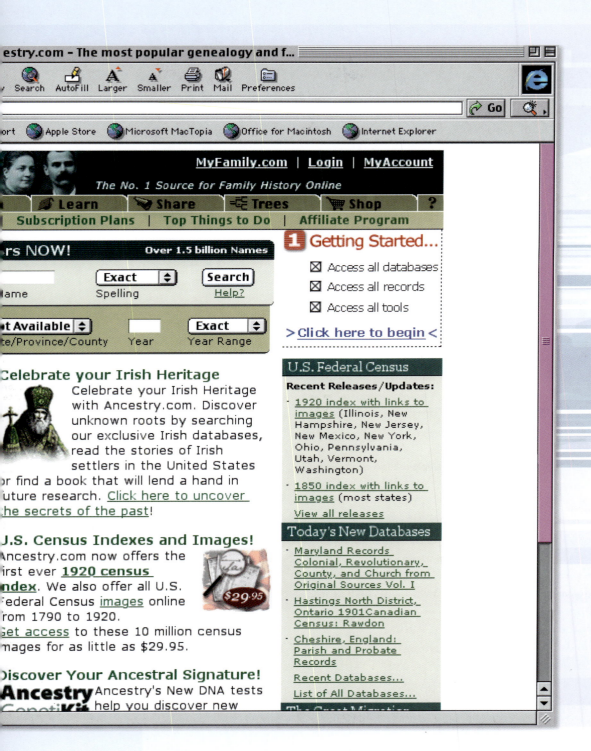

Once you've collected your information and family history documents it's finally time to start growing your tree. There are many software packages available to help you do this, but do you actually need anything other than a (potentially very large) sheet of paper—or a very long webpage? It depends on the detail you require. Pen and paper have served the genealogist for many centuries, and examples of his or her art may well be in your family history portfolio. If your tree is to be an equally simple example, then you could use conventional software applications (such as Microsoft Excel or Adobe PageMaker) to build your tree, adding in as many old and new digitized images or subsidiary information as we did in our pet calendar project (see page 48).

For a more ambitious project, dedicated family tree software has several advantages. Most significantly it can make one of the more difficult tasks in any family tree construction—reconciling all the branches of the tree—simple. And you need only enter the names of the relatives to set up your basic framework. You can instantly print out the results. Or, enter more information—facts, figures, or personal histories—relating to these. Pretty soon your tree will be blooming.

Virtually all genealogical software applications will also help you extend your search. By carefully analysing the information you've already provided (such as the names, place and date of birth, and so on), these packages can search the appropriate databases and attempt to uncover further relatives for you to investigate.

Don't underestimate the power of assisted searches such as this. For example, one of the most popular applications, Family Tree Maker, scours every genealogy-specific site currently on the Internet and finds those most likely to contain information pertinent to your searches. It can then help you study those sites for more clues to your ancestry.

Another plus point for family-tree software is its ability to track your information resources. As your tree expands, the number of resources that you've accessed in its construction can quickly grow in number, so managing them can become impossible. By keeping tabs on all the material you've searched, wasted effort is kept to a minimum.

But for most of us the mechanics of creating the tree are only of peripheral interest—we want to see the end result! And you can produce stunning family trees with photos and illustrations. Some applications even produce chronologies and timelines that show the evolution of your family, and correlate events in your family with historic milestones.

Your New Family Friend
Family-tree software delivers more than an easy way of presenting your family history. It will enhance and increase your information trawling, and give you more options on the way all that compiled data is presented.

The success of genealogy sites has meant that there is now a high perceived value in the material contained in archives. So those who are used to the free (and some might say, anarchic) nature of the Internet might be in for some surprises. Access to many archive sites (whether through direct access or via a portal) is often on a pay-per-use basis. You might be charged for accessing the data and (in some cases) charged for printing out that data. If you request a hard copy to be sent to you from the originator, you will almost certainly be charged. If you think this unfair, consider for a moment the position of the originators of this data. They do not have to place this data on the Web; in doing so they are making the work of professional researchers easier. We, as the amateur sleuths of genealogy, have to work under the same rules. And you wouldn't begrudge paying to see the real records, would you?

If you find that you are making regular visits to information resources you might find it easier to subscribe to one of the portal organizations. These charge monthly or annual subscriptions and provide unlimited access to a set or collection of databases. There are no further fees to pay. Similarly, the vendors of many family-tree software applications provide the option of purchasing their products with the bonus of subscriptions to certain databases.

Family Tree Maker—the product we discussed on page 116—includes a three-month subscription to Genealogy Library with one of its packages. This gives access to a range of researched family histories, marriage records, census indexes, and more. For a higher premium, you can include subscriptions to further databases, such as the 1900 Census and even International and Passenger Records—a vast collection of passenger lists, international censuses, and land records. But one note of caution. When you subscribe, do take care to check that those directories and databases to which you'll have access stand a good chance of being relevant. It may be of little value gaining access to the UK National Census of 1901 if your ancestry is entirely in Milwaukee, or the New York State Records if your family hails from London!

One particularly useful database to include in any subscription is World Family Tree. This is a vast searchable repository of family trees that researchers like you and me have contributed. You may be lucky and find several arms of your family already compiled in one of the trees here. Otherwise, paste yours and hope that it galvanizes others into action.

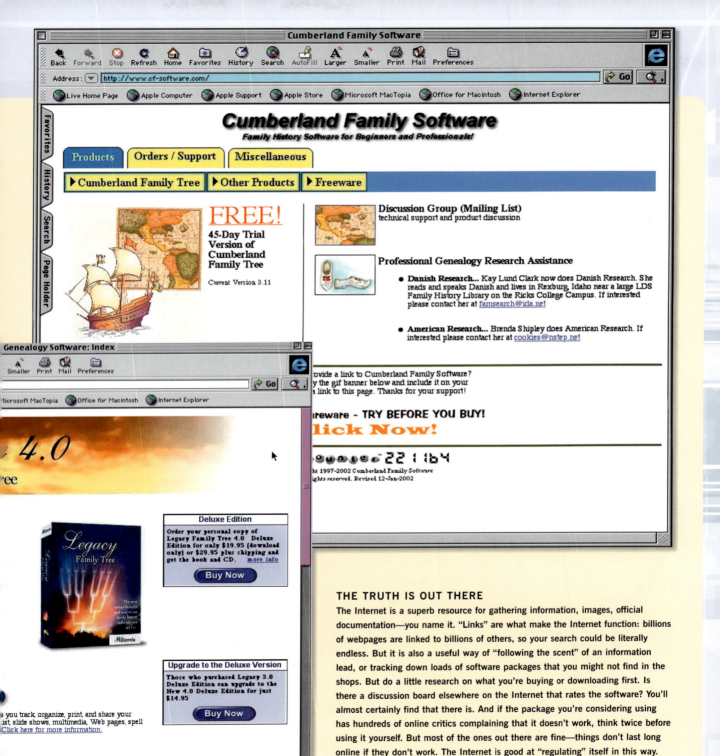

Cumberland Family Software
Family History Software for Beginners and Professionals!

Address: http://www.cf-software.com/

Live Home Page | Apple Computer | Apple Support | Apple Store | Microsoft MacTopia | Office for Macintosh | Internet Explorer

Products | Orders / Support | Miscellaneous

▶ Cumberland Family Tree | ▶ Other Products | ▶ Freeware

FREE!
45-Day Trial Version of Cumberland Family Tree

Current Version 3.11

Discussion Group (Mailing List)
technical support and product discussion

Professional Genealogy Research Assistance

- **Danish Research...** Kay Lund Clark now does Danish Research. She reads and speaks Danish and lives in Rexburg, Idaho near a large LDS Family History Library on the Ricks College Campus. If interested please contact her at famsearch@ida.net

- **American Research...** Brenda Shipley does American Research. If interested please contact her at cookies@nstep.net

...ovide a link to Cumberland Family Software?
...y the gif banner below and include it on your
...a link to this page. Thanks for your support!

...reware - TRY BEFORE YOU BUY!
...lick Now!

...221164

...t 1997-2002 Cumberland Family Software
...ights reserved. Revised 12-Jan-2002

Genealogy Software: Index

Smaller | Print | Mail | Preferences

Go

Microsoft MacTopia | Office for Macintosh | Internet Explorer

4.0
ree

Legacy Family Tree

Deluxe Edition
Order your personal copy of Legacy Family Tree 4.0 Deluxe Edition for only $19.95 (download only) or $29.95 plus shipping and get the book and CD. more info

Buy Now

Upgrade to the Deluxe Version
Those who purchased Legacy 3.0 Deluxe Edition can upgrade to the New 4.0 Deluxe Edition for just $14.95

Buy Now

...you track, organize, print, and share your
...ist, slide shows, multimedia, Web pages, spell
...Click here for more information.

...n is and much, much more. Dozens of
...ew Chronology View and report, the location
...oolbar, global spell checking, user-defined
...re Center that makes the assignment of pictures

Legacy Training

THE TRUTH IS OUT THERE

The Internet is a superb resource for gathering information, images, official documentation—you name it. "Links" are what make the Internet function: billions of webpages are linked to billions of others, so your search could be literally endless. But it is also a useful way of "following the scent" of an information lead, or tracking down loads of software packages that you might not find in the shops. But do a little research on what you're buying or downloading first. Is there a discussion board elsewhere on the Internet that rates the software? You'll almost certainly find that there is. And if the package you're considering using has hundreds of online critics complaining that it doesn't work, think twice before using it yourself. But most of the ones out there are fine—things don't last long online if they don't work. The Internet is good at "regulating" itself in this way.

Once you've done your research and built the outline family tree, you can look at embellishing the material. Photographs begged, stolen (surely not!), or borrowed (of course!) from relatives will need to be copied. As you'll remember, a simple flatbed scanner will be sufficient for digitizing most conventional photographs. But also remember that many of these—especially the older ones—will be quite fragile, so it's important to handle them with care. If the photos are mounted in an album and can't easily be removed, scan the whole album page and trim out any superfluous material later.

Time has two principal effects on your photos. It flattens the contrast through fading (which can occur even if the photos are stored in an album, away from the light), and also through the action of residual chemicals. Second, over long periods, it is almost inevitable that your photos will have suffered some physical damage. The corners get dog-eared, folds and creases develop, and, in the most severe case, the print gets torn. Fortunately all these problems can be sorted digitally! You can boost the contrast (and, on old color photos, even restore faded color) and fix all those handling marks. You can finish with a photo that is better than the original!

THE FRUITS OF THEIR LABORS

Photographs are an important element of any family tree. We've compiled an illustrated family tree for this project—and we've been fortunate to discover photographs of the great-great-grandparents of the children shown in the tree (who, we suspect, might have grandchildren of their own by now, looking at their photographs!), and we've identified all the relatives in the intervening generations. When using specialist family-tree software you'll often find that it is sufficient to save a photo to have it included in the tree. The software handles all the sizing, cropping, and placement. And notice the structure of this family tree. We could call it a "descendent" tree, as it illustrates all the descendants of the original couple, Joseph Reardon and Mary Hopkins. But you could base your tree on a selected child (for example) and trace their ancestry backward.

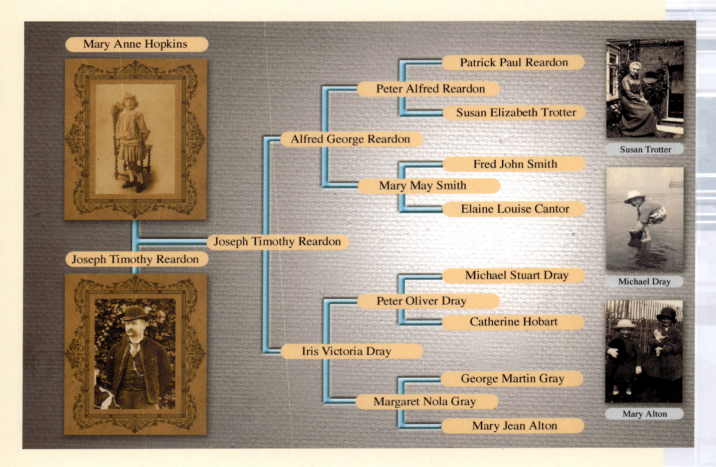

Mary Anne Hopkins

Joseph Timothy Reardon

Joseph Timothy Reardon

Alfred George Reardon

Peter Alfred Reardon

Patrick Paul Reardon

Susan Elizabeth Trotter

Mary May Smith

Fred John Smith

Elaine Louise Cantor

Iris Victoria Dray

Peter Oliver Dray

Michael Stuart Dray

Catherine Hobart

Margaret Nola Gray

George Martin Gray

Mary Jean Alton

Susan Trotter

Michael Dray

Mary Alton

Once you've created your tree you won't want to keep your research to yourself—and no doubt those curious relatives from whom you've extracted information and ephemera will be keen to see the results. Printed family trees are fine, but a family website will be much more dynamic and can grow as more and more information comes your way. Like real trees, your family tree will never be "finished"! And it will withstand the ravages of time, thanks to the digital skills you've acquired in this book. You've truly made something for future generations to enjoy!

A family website need not be just a collection of data, or a place that family members visit once to discover their own past; it can be an energetic forum through which far-flung relations can communicate, share stories, and develop a greater sense of belonging. Your website will rapidly become a family resource. It will be a place where news is shared; marriages and births announced; and biographies added. So don't be precious: that's what digital scrapbooking is all about: sharing, preserving, editing, growing... giving a new lease of life to your precious memories.

JOB DONE!

This Constance-Barry family tree website is the result of a substantial amount of research. George and Susan Barry say they have spent three years researching their ancestry and have discovered much about their ancestors, and items important to their lives.

They've avoided the pitfall of merely pasting the family tree online, by grouping the material into sensible sections. In this way, a relation can find out more by exploring the site in different ways. For example, they could use the linear family tree as the start point, and then branch off to discover more about particular relations. Or they could choose (by clicking on one of the saplings) to explore a selected time period, discovering more about the lives and times of their ancestors.

It's a site that's fun to visit, and encourages people to visit again, and even add their own stories, anecdotes, and photos. Inspired?

The English Connection!

Families are fascinated by their roots, and when those are in another country, the story is more intriguing. A short biography along with a few illustrative photos bring your ancestors to life. It's a good idea to include only a short piece of text on each page, as here, and add a good selection of image thumbnails. In this site visitors can click on each individual photo and see it enlarged to full screen. They can even print off a copy for their own album.

Home ➡

the
Constance-Barry
family tree

- *Alfred George Barry 1892-1947*

Alfred Barry was born on the 6th of July and lived for the first past of his life in <u>Rochester,</u> Kent, England. He attended Sir Joseph Williamson's Mathematical School until the outbreak of the first World War, then became a junior medical officer in France until 1918.

After the war he married <u>Victoria Hoskins</u> and moved to <u>Maidstone,</u> Kent. Victoria gave birth to <u>May</u> in 1921 and <u>Elizabeth</u> in 1923. A son, <u>Charles,</u> was born in 1926 and emigrated to the USA in 1947. *More*

Alfred Barry

Victoria Hoskins aged 9

Pictures:

1800-1900

Tea party

Victoria's home

St Luke's

Alfred's Aunts

Reginald Barry

Victoria aged 19 years

Welcome to the
Constance-Barry
family tree

Home page

Site Plan

Family Tree

Album

Surnames

News

Heirlooms

Feedback

Li...

We've spent three years researching the Constance-Barry family tree and we think that the results so far have made it all worthwhile. We hope that you agree, and if you can help us further with our searches please don't hesitate to contact us.

Some links are still nebulous but we are progressing steadily and will endeavour to update the site at least bi-monthly.

We look forward to hearing from you,

George and Susan Barry

Home ➡

1900-2000

---

the
Constance-Barry
family tree

Heirlooms

Just for fun we've included some pictures of the many artefacts handed down to us over the years. They're not particularly valuable as antiques but they mean a lot to us.

*Every item has its own little story to tell and there's a brief description accompanying the photos. If **you** have anything of interest that you would like us to feature, please don't hesitate to get in touch.* *More*

← 1800-1900 →

Richard Constance

May Barry   *Peter Barry*   *Reginald Barry*   *Jack Constance*

Keep it Light

There's a tendency for family trees to become ponderous and even academic. While much of the material might make this necessary, don't make it totally humorless. Here the Barrys have included a page of family heirlooms (with one selected by each family member) that say more about the character of each person than define the wealth of the family!

Decorative ideas: Rev those engines!

Over the next few pages, we're going to give your inspiration a kickstart with some decorative ideas for projects that could be part of a paper-based scrapbook, a website, or a CD. Then in Section 3, we'll show you how to take your ideas a step further, and recap some useful hints and tips.

If a picture's worth a thousand words, imagine what you can say in a montage. A photo record of a sporting event could be interpreted in different ways. For example, we could get that fantastic shot of a winning touchdown or the victor's celebration. Trouble is, being at the right place at the right time to take the winning shot is something even sports photographers have trouble with. Another way is a photo collage that captures the flavor of the event. Getting photos for this is usually much simpler and more practical! Remember, in real life, there are no replays.

You should aim to get as many shots as you can of different elements. The event itself is of principal importance, but don't neglect other aspects. Photos of the crowd or spectators overcome with emotion, the pre-event buildup, and amusing incidents at the sidelines will all contribute raw materials for a terrific montage. Now try different ways of combining them. Import the images into your image-editing application and create a collage. Depending on the photos, you might want to tell a story, sequencing your images so that the day's events unfold. Or create a "virtual stadium" with crowd scenes used to frame the montage of events from the field.

A Day at the Races

For this Porsche track day we wanted to convey the power and emotion of the day's racing. We took photos of the cars themselves and, by using relatively slow shutter speeds, created the impression of speed through panning and blurring. But we also took shots of details of the cars to give a more comprehensive view of the day. But creating the montage also involved a little digital trickery. Some clip-art filmstock has been used to simulate movie footage. Selected images have been pasted into the individual film frames. For the large central image, we applied a Photoshop Elements *Motion Blur* filter to the rear half of the car to suggest that the vehicle (which was parked!) was moving at high speed. For a final flourish, a close-up of a Porsche badge has been added along with a highlight. Well, even the professionals sometimes cheat, you know.

Kids at play, the big catch

It's kids' party time, so informality is the keynote of this idea. With colorful, happy shots of these little monsters, you can create an arrangement that really captures the atmosphere of the day. Spend some time getting the composition right... then spend just as long arranging and rearranging the images. That's the beauty of digital techniques: nothing's fixed until you say so. So, don't worry too much about "getting it right," but maybe start with the large images and then fill in the gaps with

progressively smaller ones. For the background, you can create this both in a bitmap package like Photoshop Elements, or in a vector drawing suite like CorelDraw. Alternatively, why not use one of the kids' own paintings as your background, and arrange the pictures on top? Above all, go for a varied selection of images. Go for full-face portrait shots; group shots; grab as much color as you can and really fill that page. And if you find you've any space, just drop another image in!

River Waveney 12/8/02 7.30am – 2.30pm Cloudy/bright Temp. 77f

Common Carp 12lb 2oz
Opposite club house, 30 yard cast, 12 ft deep swim. Moderate to fast flow.
Bait
Bread crust
Tackle
Float-leger, No 8 hook

Mirror Carp 10lb 6oz
Small island 100 yards downstream of club house, 4ft eddy, left of dead tree.
Bait
Strawberry paste
Tackle
Swim-feeder, No 8 hook

Pike 14lb 3oz
(caught by Ralph!)

Road bridge, (right of supports).
Bait
Yellow plug
Tackle
8ft rod, 12lb line

The Kids' Party

Without crafty image editing tricks we've achieved a result that looks a bit like a kids' pinboard that has been covered in photos. To further emphasize the fun nature of the project, we used a brush tool to give a big, splashy, party-style border to many of the prints. By applying bevel layer effects in Photoshop Elements, these take on a more three-dimensional effect. Splash! Now, where's Mum?

The One that Didn't Get Away

With an illustrated log book of a fishing weekend, there's less room for tall stories. A record like this says more than words could ever do. We've made a template then dropped the text and images onto it. The only image manipulation is a little cropping or resizing to ensure the photos fit the spaces. Then with bait and fish hooks ready, you've caught the day, as well as that fish!

You can just picture the day and imagine yourself dreaming by the riverside. This presentation's got it all: some lively pictures, found objects, a shot that establishes the sense of place—and all those statistics! Never again will he be able to say the fish was twice the size. Or will he? A few tweaks in your image-editing program, like Elements, and he could be holding Moby Dick instead of this less impressive beast. Go for a strong combination of graphics (from a drawing or painting application), text, and photos. It's a good idea to be economical with text. Let the pictures tell the story: even if they're stretching the truth!

House, garden, and work

A great way of showing off a prized possession whether it's an antique, a collectible, or a beautiful garden (as here) is to combine the "big picture" with smaller photos that pick out the details. But that's just the seeds of the idea; to really bring this garden into bloom, why not scan some of the plant name markers and use them as graphics to point out some of your pride and joy's best features? To make the smaller photos more prominent it's a good idea to use your

picture editing software to differentiate them from the background. You could, for example, put a drop shadow behind some of the smaller images, or tint the background (perhaps giving it an antique, sepia tone look). Here, though, we've chosen to give our main image a pale vignette to create some dynamics and movement, and to emphasize the light on this early summer's day. Turning the image into a webpage could be the beginnings of

21st June

A fine, dry month with only an occasional downpour. The azaleas and wisteria gave their best display for years, as did the lupins although they were troubled with early blackfly. Planted cuttings from Sue's garden.

Remember to spray and water day lilies if dry.

Old pruning knife found in herbaceous border. This could have belonged to Fred Collier, who gardened here before 1989.

Seven blue tits managed to avoid Daisy the cat and were successfully hatched in the nest box above the conservatory.

December 21st last year. Cold north winds brought 4" of snow. An unexpected surprise before Christmas.

something much bigger: a colorful gardening website, with a page on each of the blooms, season by season. Photo stories are a staple of many magazines and it's not too difficult to create one yourself. They are a great way of telling a story: a family day out, for example; or, as here, a typical day at work —just to remind you of what you've left behind as you put your feet up and get creative! You can always use some clip art or clip photos to provide links in the storyline. Many image-editing applications include (sometimes in their clip-art collections) speech bubbles and text boxes that you can use to put words into your characters' mouths. If yours doesn't, you can create your own using the *Elliptical Marquee* tool in Elements, or whichever editing program you choose.

Over the Garden Wall

Creating a collage using *Layers* in Photoshop Elements can really give your viewers a walk-through guide. Use this project as a start-off point for bigger ideas: a horticultural website; a month-by-month garden calendar as each bloom comes into season... even a small business website selling seeds, or gardening advice! Or just email your friends to show them how your garden grows...

The Working Day

You can make a photo story like this easily in your image-editing program (don't forget to save the whole thing as a JPEG for the Web, or a TIFF for printing), or in a desktop publishing (layout) program, or even (with a bit of patience) using a wordprocessor. Clip-art images and graphics complete the story, or you can draw your own—or scan objects like tickets, bills, or paperclips.

Before and after, and the zoo trip

Why not combine your homemaking skills with your photographic expertise in this simple "before and after" page? Combine it with the *Moving House* Web project on page 56, and really tell the story of a house transformed, or "burn" it onto CD to capture the whole experience for years to come. It's just what the professionals do: when interior designers and stylists set about transforming a room for their clients they begin by assembling a board featuring those colors, textures, and fabrics that their

clients have liked. Take a tip from this and include color paint swatches and fabric samples (scanned on your flatbed scanner) as part of the design. Of course, you don't need to restrict this idea to just a room makeover. You can use a similar composite to show the stages and end result of creating, say, a dollhouse or any modelmaking activity. The techniques are the same: just snap away with your digital camera as you go, grab those details, surprise your friends and family as they stumble around with boxes and

Changing Rooms

Rather than a simple "before and after" shot, this collage combines a large "after" image with different views of the original room. Shots of the alterations in progress have also been included to illustrate how the transformation came about. Notice how swatches of the paint and fabric selected for the new room scheme were also scanned and have been included to complete the picture.

Origin of the Species

Photo collages of wildlife collections can often degenerate into a "survival of the fittest"-style mess on the page. By keeping photos of similar fauna together and using a background appropriate for each group of subjects, images that might otherwise be confusing become much more powerful. The use of close-ups and different shaped images adds to the composition.

cans. Then assemble it all later at your leisure—while someone else does the hard work!

Collections—of any sort—make ideal subjects for digital photo collages (as we saw in project eight), but to show them to best effect requires a little more imagination. Digital imaging techniques give us a host of inspirational tools that we can employ from the simple (such as cropping selected photos into circles) through to complex blends in which disparate subjects are combined into a single scene. Another way to group like subjects into 'families' is to digitally paste them onto an appropriate background. This could be a color or a texture that makes the subject look completely in its natural habitat! Are you in yours, yet?

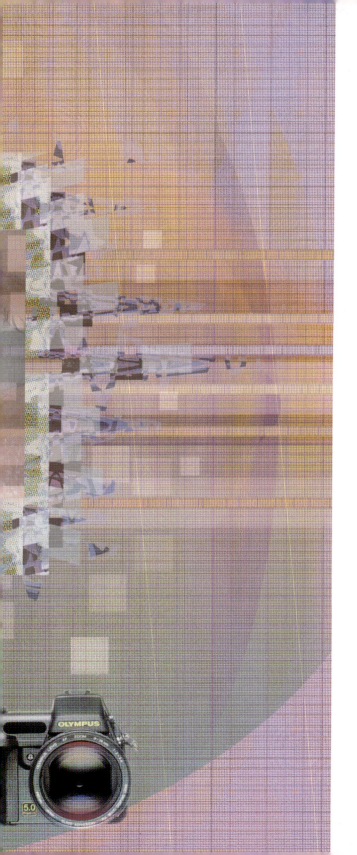

Hints and Tips

As you've worked your way through this book you'll have seen how powerful digital image editing is, and what a useful tool it is for making timeless and beautiful scrapbooks— then taking them to the next stage by publishing them online, or putting them on CD. But before embarking on any project it's a good idea to take a step back and assess the requirements of your raw material: your photos, videos, and memorabilia. Consider for a moment what needs to be done before they can grace your project. Throughout this section we'll examine issues such as these— and many more—and even look at some further uses for your masterpieces!

Taking better pictures of people

People are undoubtedly the main subjects of photography. Whether you're professional or amateur, people usually make the most compelling subjects. For most of us that compulsion is driven by emotions. We want, for example, to photograph important events, such as birthday parties and weddings that are meaningful to us. But of course it's the memories—rather than the photographs themselves—that are most important to us, so we're often indifferent to the quality of the shots we take. This is a shame, as the best photos—or the best use of those photos after the event—will take on the greatest significance as time goes by.

One of the biggest problems with photos of people is not getting in close enough. Although it might not be possible to get physically close to your subject (if they are taking part in a play or a sporting event, for example), you can make them appear larger. Use your camera's zoom lens (or switch to a telephoto lens if you are using an SLR) to ensure the subject is large in the viewfinder. If this really isn't possible, you can just select a detail of the image in your editing software and compose the picture "after the event." Shooting from a distance also makes the subjects less self-conscious, so you've a better chance of capturing their natural expressions.

It's always a good idea to shoot people using either a modest telephoto lens or a zoom lens set to an equivalent amount of magnification. Photographing people in their natural setting—whether at work or home—can also make for better portraiture, whether you're aiming for formality or informality. People are always easiest to photograph when they're at their ease, or on home territory. Taking pictures of people at work also lets you include some of the tools of their trade that add character to the shot.

Lighting

The way our subjects are lit has an important bearing on the quality of the photos. Shoot with the sun behind the subject and you tend to get a dark silhouette that professionals call "contre-jour." Portraits like this are usually unflattering, and the background is often washed out as the camera's metering system tries to adjust to the brightness of the subject. You could use flash to equalize the lighting, but still the results are rarely satisfactory. Positioning the sun behind the photographer will give you much more even lighting, but it carries the risk that, if the lighting is strong, it can cause facial shadows and makes your subject squint. The best lighting is when the source is positioned off to the sides of the photographer, though still forward of the subject. This gives sufficient shading to prevent dazzling the subject, but also produces flattering shadows.

Groups

Formal group photos have their place. Even the most avant-garde of wedding photographers feels obliged to include some "stereotypical" shots in his clients' portfolios. The problem with group shots is often not the formality of the composition, but the lack of intimacy. Getting good group shot requires the photographer and the subjects to be comfortable and relaxed with each other. Only then can warmth radiate from the photo!

Improving photographic technique

Digital image editing can—in extreme cases—turn the proverbial sow's ear into a silk purse, but it still makes good sense to get your photos right in the first place. This means ensuring that when your eye is at the camera viewfinder, you take note of and appreciate your subject. Don't click the shutter straight away (unless by hesitating you're going to miss something crucial!); check around the frame to make sure you have the best composition. Check the focus. Is the subject in focus, and if so, how much of the foreground and background do you want to be in focus too? What about the shutter speed and exposure? Are these ideally set for your subject? Here are a few tips to point you in the direction of great photos.

The Rule of Thirds

We have an instinctive desire, when photographing any subject, to place that subject at the center of the frame. We have a similar desire in landscape photography to position the horizon dead center in the frame. But neither of these is, in compositional terms, ideal. Although you shouldn't let your photography be compromised by rules, there is one very good one that can help your compositions enormously: the "rule of thirds." Divide your frame into three equal segments horizontally and vertically. When taking landscapes you'll get much better compositions when your horizon is one third down from the top (or two thirds down, if you're recording a skyscape). Similarly, a portrait is best when the eyeline is one third down. The strongest compositions of all are produced when the principal subjects are placed at the intersection of these imaginary third-lines.

Depth of Field

Any lens is capable of producing a sharp image at only one distance. Only at this distance will the subject be absolutely sharp. But by changing the size of the lens aperture we can increase this range so that those parts of the scene in front of and behind this point are also in focus. The more we close down (or "stop down") the aperture of a lens, the more of the scene that is in focus. At very small apertures it will be possible to have a wide range of distances in good focus. The drawback of using small apertures is that a correspondingly smaller amount of light is admitted, and so a much brighter scene is required unless long shutter speeds are permissible. Depth of field can be used creatively to isolate a subject from the surroundings. When the depth of field is large and much of the scene is in good focus it can sometimes be difficult to identify the intended subject. By reducing the depth of field (by using a larger aperture) we can blur the foreground and background and concentrate attention on that subject. Note that it is also possible to enhance depth-of-field effects digitally; an example is shown on page 141.

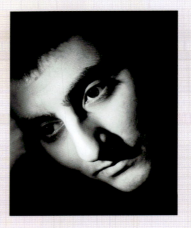

Shutter Speed

When a camera is used in *Auto* mode, we often pay scant regard to the shutter speed setting. But for some subjects—such as fast-moving vehicles and sports—it is important to get the shutter speed right. To "freeze" the action, you need to ensure the shutter speed is as high as possible. A high-speed film, such as 400 ASA, is helpful as well (specialist shops will sell you films as fast as 1600 or 3200). To blur the action (to give the impression of motion) you can use slower shutter speeds, as the portrait *above* shows. For longer shutter speeds it is usually important to use a tripod or some other kind of camera support so that the image is not spoilt by camera shake while the shutter remains open.

Exposure Control

Automatic controls also tend to adjust the camera's exposure settings so that an "average" exposure level is achieved. Although ideal for most subjects, some require different treatment. For example, photos of skiers and snow scenes photographed using normal exposure settings will be dull and muddy looking. Conversely, shots of richly colored sunsets can often become washed out as the camera compensates for the low light conditions. You can either change the settings manually or dial in an override amount, generally calibrated in "stops." Increasing the exposure will double the amount of light entering. For bright scenes, decrease the exposure by one or two stops. For dimly lit scenes, increase the exposure by a similar amount. If you are using a digital camera, preview your results. This portrait was taken with a slow exposure, with low ambient lighting and a directional spotlight.

Guide to scanning

Digital cameras have made it possible to take a photo, download it to a computer, and begin editing it within minutes. But what about all those other pictures you've taken over the years with conventional film-based cameras? And what about all that memorabilia? To edit images like these, you first need to convert each into a digital image; one that can be loaded onto your computer.

For this we need a flatbed scanner. Sometimes called "desktop" scanners, they scan photos (or flat artwork, and documents) line by line, building up a digital copy of the original in much the same way as a television works. You can set the scanner resolution to determine the amount of detail that is recorded. If you are scanning your photos to use on a webpage you need to scan at around 75 dots per inch (dpi) resolution to produce an onscreen image the same size as the original. For printed output you will need a higher resolution of 300dpi, or even 600dpi. Most scanners can scan at a much higher resolution than this to retain maximum detail. The image resolution can be changed later (optimized) for Web usage.

Where that extra resolution comes in useful is in scanning transparent media such as negatives and slides. By adding a backlight (rather than using the light built into the body of the scanner), your scanner can make digital copies of your collection of slides and negatives. It will even transform your negatives into positives in the process!

Performing a scan is simplicity itself. You place the original, face down, on the glass plate of the scanner. Press the preview button (either in the scanner software or, with a few scanner models, on the scanner itself) to produce a fast preview scan. This rough lets the scanner adjust the exposure and allows you to select a cropped area of the image. This will save time and disk space when running the final scan.

That final scan will take between a few seconds and a couple of minutes depending on the resolution selected and the area to be scanned.

Slide Scanners

Slide scanners work on a similar principle to flatbed scanners, but are optimized to scan the smaller dimensions of transparencies and negatives. Most models accommodate 35mm media and, via an adaptor, APS (Advanced Photographic System) film. Models for much larger media (medium and large format) are also available, but are generally considered professional equipment and priced accordingly. Many slide scanners feature an autoloading facility that enables the automatic scanning of batches of slides.

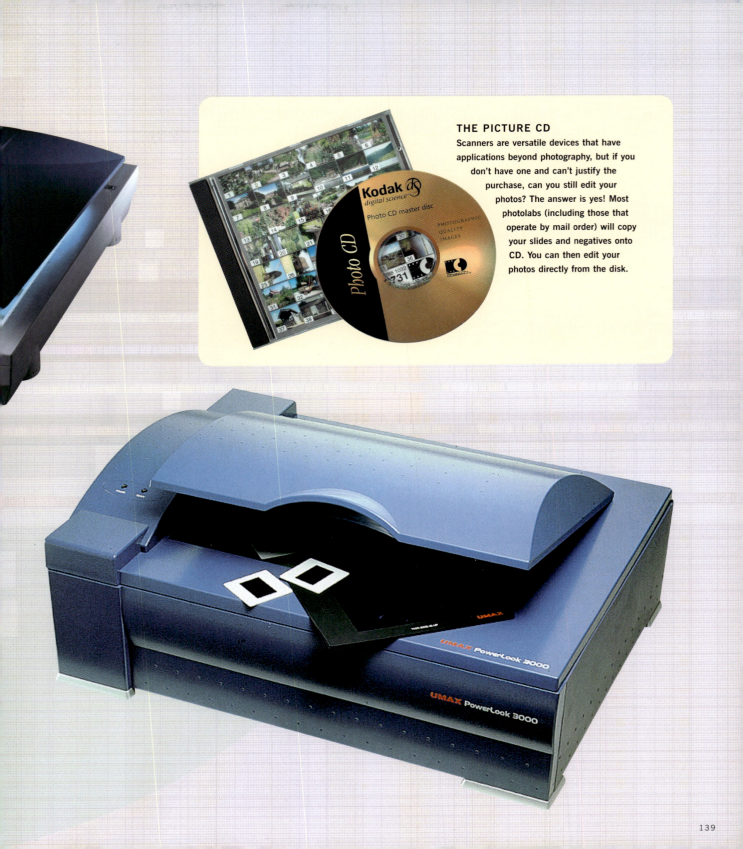

THE PICTURE CD

Scanners are versatile devices that have applications beyond photography, but if you don't have one and can't justify the purchase, can you still edit your photos? The answer is yes! Most photolabs (including those that operate by mail order) will copy your slides and negatives onto CD. You can then edit your photos directly from the disk.

Improving images

Some image problems and defects seem to occur with alarming regularity. Whether or not its through poor technique (not yours, of course!), we often end up with photos that are slightly unsharp, or perhaps have a poor color balance or even an incorrect depth of field. But the good news is that image-editing techniques let us improve these—and others—usually with a few mouse clicks, and a little application of intelligence, taste, and good judgment. Don't forget that when you are working digitally you can try any effect you wish, and if you don't like the result return to the original and begin again. So you can embark on flights of fantasy in the certain knowledge that you are not compromising your valued photo collection!

SHARPENING

Let's be clear from the start. If your photo is blurred (whether through poor focusing or camera shake) you can't restore focus digitally. However, you can restore the perceived sharpness of an image. So what's the difference? When your image is in sharp focus there will be a substantial amount of fine detail visible. When the image is only slightly out of focus, this detail is lost. So, you can use specialised filters to make the image look sharper, but you can never restore that fine detail. *Sharpen* filters work by making soft edges appear sharper by increasing the contrast on either side. They are ideal for fixing those photos that are not critically sharp, but can't do much for those photos that are simply blurred. Your image-editing application will feature several sharpening tools (designed either to sharpen the whole image or a selected part), but the most useful is one called the *Unsharp Mask*, or USM. The mechanics of this filter are rather complex so it's a good idea to play with the settings provided until you get the best sharpening effect. The standard *Sharpen* and *Sharpen More* filters are far cruder in effect, and are best reserved for test shots.

BLURRING

If you've been working hard at getting your images sharp, you're probably wondering why you'd want to blur them. In fact, you rarely need to blur an entire image, but you can get fantastic results by creatively blurring selected parts. For example, you can select and blur parts of the foreground and background to emphasize depth of field. If you want to reduce the depth of field in a photo, you can progressively blur those parts of the scene "away" from the subject. Other blur filters allow you to simulate effects such as using a motorized zoom lens to zoom out during a shot, or even blurring the wheels of a car to make a stationary vehicle appear to be moving!

COLOR QUALITY

If you were able to compare your favorite photo with the original scene you'd probably be surprised by how different the colors in your "perfect" print were in comparison. There are no absolutes when it comes to photographing the color in a scene, but our eyes and brains are pretty tolerant in accepting colors that are approximately correct. But there are limits, and we cross these often when photographing subjects that are unusually lit. Indoor scenes lit only by normal tungsten lights often take on a salmon pink tone, while fluorescent lighting can cause all manner of color casts. Sometimes we want this cast, because it might convey a certain feeling (such as "warmth" in a candle-lit scene), but more often than not we want a more neutral result. Digital-imaging software provides easy fixes to color casts. Photoshop Elements' *Color Cast* command lets the user identify part of a scene that should be white or neutral and then adjusts the colors accordingly. This is particularly useful in removing nonstandard color casts. The alternative *Color Balance* command enables the balance between colors to be manually altered. For example, reducing the amount of red and yellow in a photo will reduce the color cast due to tungsten lighting.

Retouching old photographs

Retouching old photographs has been one of the most significant advances achieved by digital imaging, and for a long time the techniques were jealously guarded. Now the mystique has been blown away, just about anyone can give old photos a second lease of life. And with the tools currently available you can achieve results that are even better than the original would have been when it was first printed.

When you digitally retouch a photo you're not doing anything to the original photo. Rather, you first scan the photo (typically using a flatbed scanner) so that you have a digital copy on your computer. Also, it means that the original photo can be returned to its album or frame and be enjoyed even after an enhanced version has been produced.

AUTO EVERYTHING

Where a photo has no physical damage but is faded or discolored, you can use automatic correction tools to effect a quick restoration. These tools (which masquerade under names like *Auto Enhance*, *Auto Fix*, or *Auto Correct*) work by analyzing the photo to determine the range of colors, tones, and brightness, then adjusting these to give an "ideal" mix. Although few photos conform to an ideal pattern, the results from using these tools are, in general, remarkably good, and some give you a range of options from which to choose. The tools won't rescue the hopeless cases, but to make quick adjustments they take some beating, and might at least make an image usable, if not picture perfect!

Before...

...and, after!

Old Retainers... Renewed!
Old photos fade, or become torn, or damaged. Even color pictures from the 1970s will be showing their age by now. But with the aid of some of the retouching techniques explored below, you can not only turn back the clock, and undo the damage... you could end up with a better picture than when it was originally taken!

The first step in retouching a photo is one of assessment. You need to look closely at the picture and establish exactly what needs to be done. Depending on the state of your original, you may need to:

- Replace missing parts. An old photograph that has been badly creased might have broken into pieces, some of which may not have been kept.

- Repair tears and creases. Even if the photo is still in one piece, there may be surface damage that needs attention.

- Remove dust and scratches. More superficial marking can be due to dust and scratch marks that might date back to the original printing of the photograph, or have accumulated over the years. There may even be some new ones due to dirt on the scanner!

- Adjust the contrast, brightness, and, if appropriate, the color. With all other damage corrected, you can boost flat contrast, alter the brightness, and even correct faded or distorted color.

The first three steps involve the *Clone* or *Rubber Stamp* tool, and/or, in the case of Photoshop 7, the *Healing Brush*. In the case of missing parts, you can sample pixels from other parts of the background to make good the missing sections, in much the same way that we used the foliage background to obscure a wedding guest in the example on page 81. Where the missing section includes part of the main subject (rather than the background) you will need to be a little more cunning and use a fine *Clone*, *Rubber Stamp*, or *Healing Brush* to paint the appropriate pixels into place.

You can attend to tears and scratch marks by cloning pixels from either side of the damage. It's a good idea to blend the colors either side of the tear. Set the tool's opacity to 50% to overpaint the original cloning work using pixels from either side to achieve this, or consider feathering, smudging, or slightly blurring the edges (see your software's instruction manual). Smaller blemishes can be attended to by simply dabbing the clone brush over the marks using nearby pixels.

Finally, adjust the contrast and brightness controls to restore the look of a pristine print. You could even try the *Sharpen* or *Unsharp Mask* filters to make the final print look even sharper than the original.

Capturing video

The main reason digital video is promoted so intensively is its quality. Promising near-broadcast quality with a high-quality video capture card (a euphemism for "very good indeed"), it is equally suited for recording family occasions as it is for semi-professional work. Other plusses include the compact size of the camera (many models are pocket-sized, if your pockets are deep enough to buy them), and the ease with which video recordings can be edited using a computer.

This is all well and good, but what if you have an analog video camera? Or what if you own a digital video camera now, but have a large collection of video recordings made on earlier, non-digital tape? No problem: you can use these tapes almost as easily.

Plug and Play

If your computer does not feature a FireWire option don't worry. It is easy to purchase and fit third-party cards. If you are not comfortable fitting one of these yourself, your local computer store can often do this—and test it—for you. Some video-editing applications are also available as "bundles" along with a compatible FireWire card.

USB Capture Devices

Although the data rate through USB connections (USB 1 or 2) makes them inappropriate for handling digital video, it is possible to transfer analog video using one. Converters such as this are designed to both transfer video recordings and to play conventional television programming on your monitor. Like conventional A to D Converters, these are bidirectional devices that also permit the outputting of edited video material.

From A to D

Compact and easy to use, A to D Converters make it simple to convert your historic collection of video recordings to digital, ready for editing. Once you've edited your video you can also copy your edited version back to the video tape ready to play on your VCR.

To edit analog video requires an extra piece of equipment known as an Analog to Digital Converter—or A to D Converter for short—which converts an analog signals into a digital one; in other words, one that your computer can understand and interpret in the same way as an original digital recording. A to D Converters come in two flavors. One, perhaps the neatest, is a computer board that is mounted inside your computer, in one of the computer's expansion slots. This provides connections for your analog video camera (or VCR) and feeds the digital signal directly into the computer.

If you don't have any expansion slots (perhaps you use a low-end laptop or a notebook computer), or you don't fancy the idea of opening your computer to insert an auxiliary card, then you'll also find external A to D Converters are widely available. These are small, desktop peripheral devices around the size of an external CD drive or CD writer. You connect your analog camera or VCR to these, but then you'll need to connect the converter to the computer, generally using a FireWire (iLink) connection.

No special video or electronic skills are needed to use them. The operation of A to D Converters varies according to model and type but many models act like—and are seen by video editing software as—digital video cameras. You can import video footage in much the same way, and with applications such as Apple's iMovie (Mac) you'll even find that scenes are divided into video clips in exactly the same way as with a digital video recording.

It's as easy as A to D!

Combining video and sound

Whether you have used digital video, or, as we described on the previous page, an A to D Converter, once you've imported your recordings and started editing, you are going to want to produce a top-notch movie. In our wedding video project we examined the ways in which we could embellish the basic edited recording by using special effects and transitions. To make our production complete we need to look more closely at the opportunities offered by video-editing applications with regard to sound.

Our edited video will already contain the original soundtrack that was recorded along with the original video. "CD quality" is the claim you'll hear over and over again for digital video sound. True, digital video as a technology is capable of recording sound to the standards of CD music recordings. However, while the sound circuitry is capable, the devices—the microphones—we use to provide the audio signal are rarely up to the standard required to reproduce sound of this quality. Built-in microphones are competent all-rounders, but like most all-rounders, excel in no one area.

So we suggest investing in an auxiliary microphone. The most useful of these are optimized both for recording sound directly ahead of the camera (where your action takes place!), but also for recording some of the sounds around it (so-called "ambient" sounds).

Once you've compiled your video, even if you have used a top-grade microphone, you'll find that scene transitions can be problematic as far as sound is concerned. When using fades and cross fades you'll find the sound fades as well to match the visuals, while the sound during ordinary, abrupt scene transitions changes equally abruptly. Obviously this is far from ideal, and will lend your video an unnecessarily "amateur" feel. Video-editing applications do often provide the means to fade the sound in a clip but often this is an equally unsatisfactory solution. A more effective solution is to use a

Sound Performance?
Given their size and positioning, the microphones built in to virtually every video camera do a remarkable job. They are something of a compromise and as such are not ideal for all occasions. There is also a strong risk that, being integral to the camera, they will pick up the sound of the camera motor and even that of the zoom lens if the latter is used during the recording.

The Auxiliary Mic
Although an auxiliary microphone adds bulk to and affects the handling of your digital movie camera, the pain is certainly worthwhile when you hear the results. Models such as this are available with standard response (that is, they are optimized to pick up those sounds immediately in front of the camera) and "zoom" response. Something of an inaccurate name, zoom models are designed with particular sensitivity for a small area in front of the camera in order to pick up more distant sound.

good piece of background music that, being recorded after the video material is edited, will be continuous and lessen the impact of any gaffs in the original soundtrack. You'll find many sources of background music on the Web including useful "looping" music that plays continuously with no obvious break. Importing these—or any sound files—to your video-editing application is simple and the imported track can be drag and dropped in the same ways as the video clips. You can even apply fades at the start and finish.

Sound Mixing

With two audio tracks (that are additional to the soundtrack already recorded with the video footage) it is easy to add background music and even sound effects. You can use the same tools as used for editing the video to achieve frame-accurate precision in the placement of the sound files.

Animation and graphics

If you want to add a little extra spice to your digital scrapbook projects, whether you're publishing them on the Web or burning them onto CD, then why not add some basic animation? It's not as daunting as it sounds. If you can generate a simple graphic, then in many software packages you can animate it too. And there's nothing to stop you scanning a kid's painting, a party hat, or even a photo of one of your friends and turning it into the raw material for a quick animation. So, imagine the kids' party project on page 126 with a clown's face bouncing across it, or a succession of images in the fishing project on page 127, showing the catch being lifted out of the water!

Animations are perhaps the most obvious attention-grabbing features on websites, and are easily constructed in applications like ImageReady, Macromedia Fireworks, and Corel PhotoPaint, or in dedicated (and complex) software such as Macromedia Flash. As you've surfed through websites, you'll probably have seen that animations can vary from the simple and basic, through to complex, virtual environments. The most common format is GIF animation.

GIF, or Graphics Interchange Format, permits animation and although it is not best suited to handling photos, can greatly compress graphics, making it the format ideal for simple, animated graphics.

A FLASHY ALTERNATIVE

GIF animations are often perceived as being rather basic in their results, and lackluster in their animation. This is largely untrue; some truly spectacular animations have been produced in this format. But for the best in animation you'll need to use Macromedia's superb animation tool Flash, which is also the name for the underlying technology. You'll need to buy a copy of this program and spend some time studying the construction process, but the results will amply repay your efforts.

ROLLOVERS

You've probably made good use of website rollovers without realizing exactly what they are. Remember those "hotspots" on a website, where hovering your pointer over them, or clicking your mouse, would change the underlying text to a different color, or change the graphic in some way, such as to a "pressed button" effect. That's a rollover. They are used to acknowledge that you're on an area of the website that is linked to another, and that by clicking on it that link will be activated. The imaginative website creator won't be happy with a simple change of color for a rollover; they'll want something more dramatic—and will probably want the rollover to change again once the mouse has been clicked. You can create exciting rollovers in much the same way as a GIF animation. Using the *Rollover* palette in ImageReady, for example, you can determine the look of the rollover for *Normal, Mouseover, Mouseclicked*, and other states.

GIF ANIMATIONS

GIF animations are widely seen across the Web largely on account of the tool available to create them. Adobe Photoshop includes an animation generator in its companion product ImageReady, while Paintshop Pro (Win only) features Animation Shop, a separate product dedicated to the creation of GIF animations. You produce a GIF animation as you would a conventional cartoon animation, laying down "cels" that correspond to each individual still frame of the animation. When these are displayed in rapid succession, they create the illusion of movement. You can create a series of cels either by creating a sequence of images, or by modifying an original image in some way. The latter is more space efficient and leads to a more compact animation. Most animation tools also allow you to "tween," which is where the software generates the "in-between" images of a sequence automatically. You can then specify how the animation plays, determine how long each cel is displayed for, and whether the animation plays once, a set number of times, or indefinitely.

Outputting to nontraditional media

PERFECT PHOTOS

SUPERB SCANNING

RIGHTING WRONGS

JUST A RETOUCH?

CATCH THAT VIDEO!

SOUND AND VISION

GET ANIMATED

▶ NOW BUY THE T-SHIRT

Digital images have a wide range of applications, as you've seen throughout this book. You can write them to CD, or even DVD; paste them on a website; email them to your friends and family, or compile a truly innovative scrapbook from your efforts, with just a little imagination and confidence.

But as you know, digital means infinitely editable, and once something has been digitized and turned into all those exciting ones and zeros that can be sent from one side of the globe to the other in a matter of seconds, you'll discover that it can be output onto a thousand and one different things.

For example, decal papers enable an image to be printed onto fabric, such as onto a T-shirt, simply by ironing over the back of the paper. Many inkjet printers feature a special setting for decal paper that ensures the correct amount of ink is laid onto the paper, and that the photo is printed in reverse—ready to be used.

Similar decal papers are produced for immortalizing your image on mugs and plates, and a variety of other surfaces. As you might expect, dozens of online services, not to mention outlets in your local shopping mall, have sprung up to take advantage of this. Many of the big Web "portals," such as Yahoo!, offer just such a service. So, if you surf or shop around, you'll discover you can get your favorite images onto mousemats, bed linen, posters, bibs, baby clothes, and even office stationery items such as notelet holders, pens, and rulers.

Perfect for the last-minute gift!

Gifts Galore!
Remember all those photo-based gifts that your local photofinisher or minilab used to offer to create from your best negatives? Well, all these and much, much more are available from your digital shots too, and many of them can be ordered online. Jigsaw puzzles, place mats, and coasters are bestsellers, but poster-sized prints are becoming increasingly popular as well.

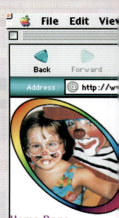

Mugshots

Transferring a photo image to a mug or other piece of china is a great way to use your best photos. You can have these made direct from your digital files via your local photo lab, online, or you can do the job yourself. In either case remember to follow any instructions supplied precisely. You'll find some products are dishwasher proof, but others less so, to put it tactfully; some are also less resilient to detergents! So, be careful with your new family heirlooms...

File   Edit   View   Go   Favorites   Tools   Window   Help   Internet Explorer

Custom Photo Gift Items

Back   Forward   Stop   Refresh   Home   AutoFill   Print   Mail

Address: http://www.imagineyourphotos.com/index2.htm   › go

Home Page
Order Instructions

Monthly Special
Products

Photo Lab &
Retailer Programs
Photo Gift PAcK's
Corporate Sales

FAQ
Our Guarantee
Our Story
Customer Comments

Your Personalized Photo Coffee Mug

Available with your photo, personalized message or logo. White only. 11-ounce ceramic mug, microwave and dishwasher safe. Waterproof.
$15.95 each

Click Here   BUY IT   Add to Cart

Check Your Shopping Basket

All items are shipped within 5 business days after receipt of order. Quality depends on your photo or image. For best results choose only bright, well focused, photos. Your original photo or image is always returned with your ordered item(s). Shipping and Handling is $2.00 for entire order.

Personalized Photo Mouse Pads / Personalized Photo T-Shirt / Personalized Photo Mugs / Personalized Photo Tote Bags | Personalized Photo Clocks | Personalized Photo Caps | Personalized Photo Magnets | Personalized Photo Music ...shirts | Personalized Photo Aprons | Personalized Photo ...Photo Baby's First Photo Albums | Personalized Photo ...Photo Pillow Cases | Special of the Month

...nc. All Rights Reserved

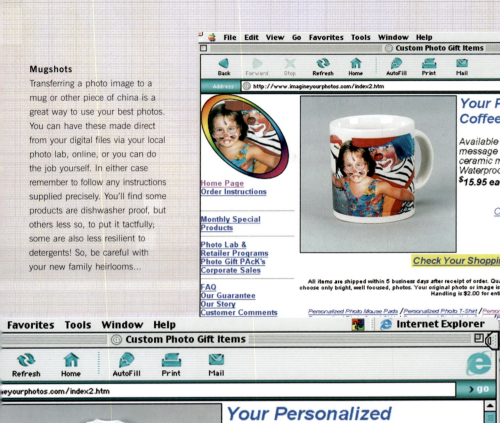

Favorites   Tools   Window   Help   Internet Explorer

Custom Photo Gift Items

Refresh   Home   AutoFill   Print   Mail

...eyourphotos.com/index2.htm   › go

Your Personalized Photo T-Shirt

Available with your photo, personalized message or logo. White Hanes Beefy-T 100% cotton. Keeps you warm in winter and cool in summer. Available in youth and adult sizes.
$15.95 each

Click the Button for the size you want:

Adult Sizes:	Youth Sizes:
○ Adult Small	○ Youth Small (6-8)
○ Adult Medium	○ Youth Medium (10-12)
○ Adult Large	○ Youth Large (14-16)
○ Adult Extra Large	

Click Here to   BUY IT   Add to Cart

Get it on your Chest

Personalized T-shirts featuring your favorite photos or even your own graphics are easy to produce at home in small numbers, or you can order them in larger quantities from a specialist supplier for parties, trips, and so on. And because it's possible to transfer your print to any cotton-based products, you needn't limit yourself to just T-shirts. Kids' clothes or bed linen are possible targets for your work (but make sure you test on a small piece of material to test its willingness to accept the inks).

Glossary (the helpful science bit)

Adobe Inc US company that develops software for specialist, creative tasks such as Web design, graphic design, and video editing. Its products are widely used by both professionals and amateurs. Photoshop, Photoshop Elements, and the video editing package Premiere are some of its most successful software products.

animated GIF A GIF file containing more than one image. Many programs, including Web browsers, will display each of the images in turn, thus producing an animation.

animation The process of creating a moving image by rapidly moving from one still image to the next. Animations are now commonly created by means of specialist software that renders sequences in a variety of formats, typically QuickTime, AVI, and animated GIF.

antialias/antialiasing The technique of optically eliminating the jagged effect of bitmapped images or text reproduced on low-resolution devices such as monitors.

Apple Computer US-based computer company whose Apple Macintosh computer ("the Mac") was at the forefront of the computing revolution in the 1980s. Its iMac range of computers has revived the company's fortunes in recent years, and its products are still the computers of choice in industries such as publishing, media and advertising (which use them mainly for design-led work). A Mac, though broadly similar, is not the same as a Windows PC, so software designed *solely* for one type of machine will not run successfully on the other Many popular software packages are available for both platforms, however. Ask your retailer.

attribute The specification applied to a character, box, or other item in a design, layout or image editing application. Character attributes include font, size, style, color, shade, scaling, kerning, and so on.

authoring tool/application/ program Software that creates text, drawing, painting, animation, and audio features, and combines these with a scripting language that determines how each element of a page behaves when published on the Internet.

bevel In image-editing software, a chamfered edge that can be applied to type, buttons, or selections to emphasize a three-dimensional effect.

bitmap An array of values specifying the color of every pixel in a digital image.

bitmapped font One in which the characters are made up of dots, or pixels, as distinct from an outline font, which is drawn from vectors. Bitmapped fonts generally accompany PostScript Type 1 fonts and are used to render the fonts' shapes onscreen.

bitmapped graphic An image made up of dots, or pixels, and usually produced by painting or image-editing applications (as distinct from the vector images of "object-oriented" drawing applications).

body One of the main structures of an HTML document, falling between the header and the footer.

brightness The strength of luminescence from light to dark.

browser/Web browser Program that enables the viewing or "browsing" of World Wide Web pages across the Internet. The most commonly used browsers are Netscape's Navigator and Microsoft's Internet Explorer. Version numbers are important, as these indicate the level of HTML that the browser supports. Another browser, "Opera," is competitive because of its compact size, efficient performance, and security. It is rapidly gaining popularity.

burn(ing) The act of recording data onto a CD in a CD burner (recorder). Software such as Roxio's Toast (Mac) is used for this task when recording from a computer to an external device.

CD-ROM CD (Compact Disk) Read-Only Memory. An evolution of the CD allowing the storage of up to 600 Megabytes of data, such as images, video clips, text and other digital files. But the disks are "Read only," which means the user can't edit or overwrite the data.

CD-R / CD-RW CD Recordable / CD-ReWriteable. CD-Rs are inexpensive disks on which you can store any digital data, or roughly 77 minutes of audio (on a hi-fi CD recorder). But once written and finalized (fixed), the data cannot be erased, edited or modified. Similar to the above, CD-RW disks can be "unfinalized" then overwritten, in part or entirely, any number of times. However, CD-RWs will not play on every type of device—a CD-RW recorded on a hi-fi type of CD recorder will not play on most other CD players.

clip-art/clip media Collections of (usually) royalty-free photographs, illustrations, design devices, and other pre-created items, such as movies, sounds, and 3D wireframes.

clone/cloning In most image-editing packages, Clone tools allow the user to sample pixels (picture elements) from one part of an image, such as a digital photograph, and use them to "paint" over other areas of the image. The process is useful for removing unwanted parts of an image, or correcting problems, such as closed eyes if the subject blinked while being photographed. In Photoshop and Photoshop Elements, the tool is known as the Rubber Stamp.

color picker The term describing a color model when displayed on a computer monitor. Color pickers may be specific to an application such as Adobe Photoshop, a third-party color model such as PANTONE, or to the operating system running on your computer.

Composer A simple webpage-building package that comes with the Netscape browser.

compression The technique of rearranging data so that it either occupies less space on disk, or transfers faster between devices or over communication lines. For example, high-quality digital images, such as photographs, can take up an enormous amount of disk space, transfer slowly, and use a lot of processing power. They need to be compressed (the file size needs to be made smaller) before they can be published on the Web, as otherwise they would take too long to appear onscreen. But

compressing them can lead to a loss of quality. Compression methods that do not lose data are referred to as "lossless," while "lossy" describes methods in which some data is lost.

contrast The degree of difference between adjacent tones in an image from the lightest to the darkest. "High contrast" describes an image with light highlights and dark shadows, but with few shades in between; while a "low contrast" image is one with even tones and few dark areas or highlights. These settings are usually editable.

copyright The right of a person who creates an original work to protect that work by controlling how and where it may be reproduced.

copyright-free A misnomer used to describe ready-made resources, such as clip-art. In fact, these resources are rarely, if ever, "copyright free." Generally it is only the licence to use the material which is granted by purchase. "Royalty free" is a more accurate description.

digitize To convert anything, for example, text, images, or sound, into binary form so that it can be digitally processed. In other words, transforming analog data into digital data.

dingbat The modern name for fonts of decorative symbols,

traditionally called printer's "ornaments," or "arabesques."

domain name system/service (DNS) The description of a website's "address"—the means by which you find or identify a particular website, much like a brand name or trademark. A website address is actually a number that conforms to the numerical Internet protocol (IP) addresses that computers use for information exchange, but names are far easier for us to remember. Domain names are administered by the InterNIC organization and include at least two parts: the "subdomain," typically a company or organization; and the "high-level domain," which is the part after the first dot, such as in ".com" for commercial sites, ".org" for non-profit sites, ".gov" for governmental sites, ".edu" for educational sites, and so on.

dots per inch (dpi) A unit of measurement used to represent the resolution of devices such as printers and imagesetters and also, erroneously, monitors and images, whose resolution should more properly be expressed in pixels per inch (ppi). The closer the dots or pixels (the more there are to each inch) the better the quality. Typical resolutions are 72 ppi for a monitor, 600 dpi for a laser printer, and 2,450 dpi (or more) for an imagesetter.

download To transfer data from a remote computer, such as an Internet server, to your own. The opposite of upload.

Dreamweaver Advanced website design software, made by Macromedia, and regarded as the industry standard for professional and semi-professional users.

drop shadow A shadow projected onto the background behind an image or character, designed to "lift" the image or character off the surface.

DVD Digital Video (or Versatile) Disk. Similar in appearance to CDs and CD-ROMs, DVDs have a storage capacity of up to 18 Gigabytes, far higher than CD-ROMs (600 Megabytes), and can deliver data at a higher rate. This allows DVDs to store up to 10 hours of high-quality MPEG-2 video, and more than 30 hours of medium-quality (more highly compressed) MPEG-1 video footage. DVD drives (players) are becoming standard on many new PCs, and DVD writers will become far less expensive in the near future.

dynamic HTML/DHTML (Dynamic HyperText Markup Language) A development of HTML that enables users to add enhanced features such as basic animations and highlighted buttons to webpages without having to rely on browser plugins.

export A feature provided by many applications to allow you to save a file in a format so that it can be used by another application or on a different operating system. For example, an illustration created in a drawing application may be exported as an EPS file so that it can be used in a page-layout application.

extract A tool and a process in many image-editing applications, such as Photoshop Elements, which allows the selection of part of an image (using the selection tools) and the removal of areas around it, so the subject is extracted from the picture.

eyedropper tool In some applications, a tool for gauging the color of adjacent pixels.

face Traditionally the printing surface of any metal type character, but nowadays used as a series or family name for fonts with similar characteristics, such as "modern face."

file extension The term describing the abbreviated suffix at the end of a filename that describes either its type (such as .eps or .jpg) or origin (the application that created it, such as .qxp for QuarkXPress files).

file format The way a program arranges data so that it can be stored or displayed on a computer. Common file formats are TIFF and JPEG for bitmapped image files, EPS for object-oriented image files and ASCII for text files.

File Transfer Protocol (FTP) A standard system for transmitting files between computers, across the Internet, or over a network. Although most Web browsers incorporate FTP capabilities, dedicated FTP applications offer greater flexibility. Typically, when creating a webpage, an FTP application will be used to "upload" (send) this to the Web so other people can look at it.

Flash A technology and a software package developed by Macromedia for creating simple and highly complex animations on webpages.

frame (1) A way of breaking up a scrollable browser window on a webpage into several independent windows.

frame (2) A single still picture from a movie or animation sequence. Also a single complete image from a TV picture.

FrontPage Express A cutdown version of Microsoft's webpage building software, which was bundled free with some versions of the Internet Explorer browser.

font Set of characters sharing the same typeface and size.

font file The file of a bitmapped or screen font, usually residing in a suitcase file on Mac computers.

form A special type of webpage which provides users with the means to input information directly into the website. Form pages are often used to collect information about visitors, or as a way of collecting password and username data before allowing access to secure areas.

GIF (Graphics Interchange Format) One of the main bitmapped image formats used on the Internet. GIF is a 256-color format with two specifications, GIF87a and, more recently, GIF89a, the latter providing additional features such as the use of transparent backgrounds. The GIF format uses a "lossless" compression technique, or "algorithm," and thus does not squeeze files as much as the JPEG format, which is "lossy". For use in Web browsers JPEG is the format of choice for tone images, such as photographs, while GIF is more suitable for line images and other graphics.

graduation/gradation/ gradient The smooth transition from one color/tone to another. The relationship of reproduced

lightness values to original lightness values in an imaging process, usually expressed as a tone curve.

home page The main, introductory page on a website, usually with a title and tools to navigate through the rest of the site. Also known as the index page or doorway.

host A networked computer that provides services to anyone who can access it, such as for email, file transfer, and access to the Web. When you connect to the Internet, and select a website, information will be transferred to you from the host's computer. Users' computers that request services from a host are often referred to as "clients."

HSL (Hue, Saturation, Lightness) A color model based upon the light transmitted either in an image or in your monitor—hue being the spectral color (the actual pigment color), saturation being the intensity of the color pigment (without black or white added), and brightness representing the strength of luminance from light to dark (the amount of black or white present). Variously called HLS (hue, lightness, saturation), HSV (hue, saturation, value), and HSB (hue, saturation, brightness).

hue A color found in its pure state in the spectrum.

HTML (HyperText Markup Language) The code that websites are built from. HTML is not a programming language as such, but a set of "tags" that specify type styles and sizes, the location of graphics, and other information required to construct a webpage. To provide for increasingly complex presentations such as animation, sound, and video, the basic form of HTML is seeded with miniature computer programs, or applets.

HTML table A grid on a webpage consisting of rows and columns of cells allowing precise positioning of text, pictures, movie clips, or any other element. A table can be nested within another table. Tables offer a way of giving the appearance of multi-column layouts. They can be visible, with cells framed by borders, or invisible and used only to demarcate areas containing the elements on the page. A table is specified in terms of either a pixel count, which fixes its size irrespective of the browser or screen resolution used to view it, or as a percentage of the available screen space, allowing resizing to fit the browser window.

Hypertext Transfer Protocol (http) A text-based set of rules by which files on the World Wide Web are transferred, defining the commands that Web browsers use to communicate with Web servers. The vast majority of World Wide Web addresses, or "URLs," are prefixed with "http://".

icon A onscreen graphical representation of an object (such as a disk, file, folder, or tool) or a concept, used to make identification and selection easier.

image map An image that features a set of embedded links to other documents or websites. These are activated when the mouse is clicked on the appropriate area. Often the "front page" of a website contains such a map.

image slicing The practice of dividing up a digital image into rectangular areas or slices, which can then be optimized or animated independently for efficient Web presentation. Programs that enable you to slice images automatically generate an HTML code that puts the slices back together on a webpage.

index page The first page of any website that is selected automatically by the browser if it is named "default.htm," "default.html," "index.htm," or "index.html."

interactive Any activity that involves an immediate and reciprocal action between a person and a machine (for example, driving a car), but more commonly describing dialog between a computer and its user.

interface This is a term most often used to describe the screen design that links the user with the computer program or website. The quality of the user interface often determines how well users will be able to navigate their way around the pages within the site.

Internet The world-wide network of computers linked by telephone (or other connections), providing individual and corporate users with access to information, companies, newsgroups, discussion areas, and much more.

ISP (Internet Service Provider) An organization that provides access to the Internet. At its most basic this may be a telephone number for connection, but most ISPs provide email addresses and webspace for new sites.

JPEG, JPG The Joint Photographics Experts Group. An ISO (International Standards Organization) group that defines compression standards for bitmapped color images. The abbreviated form, pronounced "jay-peg," gives its name to a "lossy" (meaning some data may be lost) compressed file format in which the degree of compression from high compression and low quality, to low compression and high quality, can be defined by the user.

kerning The adjustment of spacing between two characters (normally alphanumeric) to improve the overall look of the text.

keyline A line drawing indicating the size and position of an illustration in a layout.

layout A drawing that shows the general appearance of a design, indicating, for example, the position of text and illustrations. The term is also used when preparing a design for reproduction, and to describe the way a page is constructed in desktop publishing programs.

link A pointer, such as a highlighted piece of text in an HTML document or multimedia presentation, or an area on an image map, which takes the user to another location, page, or screen just by clicking on it.

lossless/lossy Refers to the data-losing qualities of different compression methods. "Lossless" means that no image information is lost; "lossy" means that some (or much) of the image data is lost in the compression process (but the data will download quicker).

Macromedia A software company specialising in Web design, graphics and animation packages.

Microsoft The world's leading software company, whose Windows software for the IBM-compatible PC is now installed on the vast majority of the world's computers. Its Office package, includes Word (the leading wordprocessing package), Excel (the leading spreadsheet and accounting package), and Powerpoint (the slideshow and presentation package). These are also available for the Mac. Recent versions of Windows include the Internet Explorer browser. Despite its success, the company has been accused by rivals of uncompetitive behaviour by including so many of its software packages with new PCs—a charge Microsoft refutes.

midtones/middletones The range of tonal values in an image anywhere between the darkest and lightest, usually referring to those approximately halfway.

multimedia Any combination of various digital media, such as sound, video, animation, graphics, and text, incorporated into a software product or presentation.

paragraph In an HTML document, a markup tag <P> that is used to define a new paragraph in text.

palette This term refers to a subset of colors that are needed to display a particular image. For instance, a GIF image will have a palette containing a maximum of 256 individual and distinct colors.

pixel (picture element) The smallest component of any digitally generated image, including text, such as a single dot of light on a computer screen. In its simplest form, one pixel corresponds to a single bit: 0 = off, or white, and 1 = on, or black. In color or grayscale images or monitors, one pixel may correspond to several bits. An 8-bit pixel, for example, can be displayed in any of 256 colors (the total number of different configurations that can be achieved by eight 0s and 1s).

plugin Subsidiary software for a browser or other package that enables it to perform additional functions, e.g., play sound, movies, or video.

raster(ization) Deriving from the Latin word "rastrum," meaning "rake," the method of displaying (and creating) images employed by video screens, and thus computer monitors, in which the screen image is made up of a pattern of several hundred parallel lines created by an electron beam "raking" the screen from top to bottom at a speed of about

one–sixtieth of a second. An image is created by varying the intensity of the beam at successive points along the raster. The speed at which a complete screen image, or frame, is created is called the "frame" or "refresh" rate.

rasterize(d) To rasterize is to electronically convert a vector graphics image into a bitmapped image. This may introduce aliasing, but is often necessary when preparing images for the Web; without a plug-in, browsers can only display GIF, JPEG, and PNG image files.

resolution The degree of quality, definition, or clarity with which an image is reproduced or displayed, for example in a photograph, or via a scanner, monitor screen, printer, or other output device.

resolution (2): monitor resolution, screen resolution The number of pixels across by pixels down. The three most common resolutions are 640 x 480, 800 x 600, and 1,024 x 768. The current standard Web page size is 800 x 600.

RGB (Red, Green, Blue) The primary colors of the "additive" color model, used in video technology, computer monitors, and for graphics such as for the Web and multimedia that will not ultimately be printed by the four-color (CMYK) process.

CMYK stands for "Cyan, Magenta, Yellow, BlacK".

rollover The rapid substitution of one or more images when the mouse pointer is rolled over the original image. Used extensively for navigation buttons on webpages and multimedia presentations.

rollover button A graphic button type that changes in appearance when the mouse pointer moves over it.

scanner An electronic device that converts photographic prints, objects or printed text into digital files by reading them with a beam of light.

scan(ning) An electronic process that converts a hard copy of an image into digital form by sequential exposure to a moving light beam, such as a laser. The scanned image can then be manipulated by a computer or output to separated film.

shareware Software available through user groups, magazine cover disks, etc. Although shareware is not "copy protected," it is protected by copyright and a fee is normally payable for using it, unlike "freeware."

software Computer programs that you can buy, then install into your computer (usually via CD or the

Internet), that enable your computer to perform specific tasks, such as photo editing, graphic design, and video editing. Most recent Windows PC and Apple Mac machines (such as the iMac) come with numerous basic software packages already installed. Free software (known as "freeware" or, in some circumstances, "shareware") is also available over the Internet, or on the free CDs that come with many magazines. Software is frequently "upgraded" by the manufacturer, adding new levels of functionality. Keep your eyes and ears open!

text path In many graphic design, page layout and design software packages, an invisible line—straight, curved, or irregular—along which text can be forced to flow.

thumbnail A small representation of an image used mainly for identification purposes in an image directory listing or, within Photoshop, for illustrating channels and layers. Thumbnails are also produced to accompany PictureCDs, PhotoCDs and most APS and 35-mm films submitted for processing.

TIFF, TIF (Tagged Image File Format) A standard and popular graphics file format originally developed by Aldus (now merged with Adobe) and Microsoft, used for scanned, high-resolution, bitmapped images and for color

separations. The TIFF format can be used for black-and-white, grayscale, and color images, which have been generated on different computer platforms.

tile, tiling Repeating a graphic item and placing the repetitions side-by-side in all directions so that they form a pattern.

transparency Allows a GIF image to be blended into the background by ridding it of unwanted background color.

tween(ing) A contraction of "in-between." An animator's term for the process of creating transitional frames to fill in-between key frames in an animation.

typeface The term (based on "face"—the printing surface of a metal type character) describing a type design of any size, including weight variations on that design such as light and bold, but excluding all other related designs such as italic and condensed. As distinct from "type family," which includes all related designs, and "font," which is one design of a single size, weight, and style. Thus "Baskerville" is a type family, while "Baskerville Bold" is a typeface and "9 pt Baskerville Bold Italic" is a font. (But if you use either "font" or "typeface" to describe any of the above, no-one will mind!)

Uniform Resource Locator (URL) The unique address of every webpage on the WWW. Every resource on the Internet has a unique URL which begins with letters that identify the resource type, such as "http" or "ftp" (determining the communication protocol to be used), followed by a colon and two forward slashes.

vector A mathematical description of a line that is defined in terms of physical dimensions and direction. Vectors are used in drawing packages (and Photoshop 6 upwards) to define shapes (vector graphics) that are position- and size-independent.

vector graphics Images made up of mathematically defined shapes, such as circles and rectangles, or complex paths built out of mathematically defined curves. Vector graphics images can be displayed at any size or resolution without loss of quality, and are easy to edit because the shapes retain their identity, but they lack the tonal subtlety of bitmapped images. Because vector graphics files are typically small, they are well suited to Web animation.

webpage A published HTML document on the World Wide Web, which when linked with others, forms a website, along with other files, such as graphics.

Web server A computer ("host") that is dedicated to Web services.

website The address, location (on a server), and collection of documents and resources for any particular interlinked set of webpages.

Word The world's leading wordprocessing package, developed by Microsoft for the PC and the Mac. Although designed for creating letters and documents, Word includes simple webpage building functions within its "Save as HTML" function, found under the "File" menu.

World Wide Web (WWW) The term used to describe the entire collection of Web servers all over the world that are connected to the Internet. The term also describes the particular type of Internet access architecture that uses a combination of HTML and various graphic formats, such as GIF and JPEG, to publish formatted text that can be read by Web browsers. Colloquially termed simply "the Web" or, rarely, by the shorthand "W3."

World Wide Web Consortium (W3C) The global organization that is largely responsible or maintaining and managing standards across the Web. It is chaired by the UK's Tim Berners Lee, progenitor of the Web.

BOOKS: DIGITAL PHOTOGRAPHY

The Complete Guide to Digital Photography
Michael Freeman
Silver Pixel Press
ISBN 1-883403-91-X

Digital Imaging for Photographers
Adrian Davies & Phil Fennessy
Focal Press
ISBN 0-240-51590-0

Digital Photography: A Basic Guide to New Technology
Jenni Bidner
Kodak Books
ISBN 0-87985-797-8

Real World Digital Photography
Deke McClelland &
Katrin Eismann
Peachpit Press
ISBN 0-201-35402-0

Start with a Digital Camera
John Odam
Peachpit Press
ISBN 0-201-35424-1

BOOKS: SOFTWARE

Adobe Photoshop 6.0 for Photographers
Martin Evening
Focal Press
Oxford UK, 2001

Easy Adobe Photoshop 6
Kate Binder
Que
Indianapolis, 2001

Paintshop Pro 7 in Easy Steps
Stephen Copestake
Computer Step
Warwickshire UK, 2001

Paintshop Pro 7 Explained
N. Kantaris
Bernard Babani (Publishing)
London 2001

WEBSITES: DIGITAL IMAGING, PHOTOGRAPHY

Note that website addresses can change, and sites can appear and disappear almost daily. Use a search engine to help you find new arrivals or check addresses.

The Complete Guide to Digital Photography
www.completeguidetodigitalphotography.com

Creativepro
("news and resources for creative professionals")
www.creativepro.com

The Digital Camera Resource Page
(consumer-oriented resource)
www.dcresource.com

Digital Photography
(news and reviews)
www.digital-photography.org

Digital Photography Review
www.dpreview.com

ePHOTOzine
www.ephotozine.com

The Imaging Resource
(news and reviews)
www.imaging-resource.com

Photolink International
(education in photography and related fields)
www.photoeducation.net

photo.net
(photography resource site: community, advice, gallery, tutorials)
www.photo.net

ShortCourses: Digital Photography: Theory and Practice
www.shortcourses.com

WEBSITES: SOFTWARE

Paintshop Pro
www.jasc.com

PhotoImpact, PhotoExpress
www.ulead.com

Photo-Paint, CorelDRAW!
www.corel.com

Photoshop, Photoshop Elements, ImageReady, Illustrator
www.adobe.com

Photosuite
www.mgisoft.com

Picture Publisher
www.micrografx.com